At Home in Diaspora

SOUTH ASIAN SCHOLARS
AND THE WEST

T0364989

At Home in Diaspora

SOUTH ASIAN SCHOLARS
AND THE WEST

edited by
Jackie Assayag
and
Véronique Bénéï

INDIANA
University Press
Bloomington & Indianapolis

This book is a publication of

Indiana University Press
601 North Morton Street
Bloomington, Indiana 47404-3797 USA

http://iupress.indiana.edu

Telephone orders   800-842-6796
Fax orders   812-855-7931
Orders by e-mail   iuporder@indiana.edu

Published in South Asia by Permanent Black
D-28 Oxford Apts, 11 IP Extension, New Delhi 110092

This edition is for sale outside South Asia
by arrangement with Permanent Black

Library of Congress Cataloging-in-Publication Data

At home in diaspora : South Asian scholars and the West / edited by Jackie
Assayag and Véronique Bénéï.
       p. cm.
Includes bibliographical references and index.
   ISBN 0-253-34332-1 (cloth : alk. paper)—ISBN 0-253-21636-2 (pbk. : alk.
paper)
   1. South Asia—Study and teaching—United States. 2. South Asia—Study and
teaching—Europe. 3. Scholars—South Asia—Biography. 4. Scholars—United
States—Biography. •5. Scholars—Europe—Biography. I. Assayag, Jackie. •II.
Bénéï, Véronique.
   DS339.9.U6A89 2003
   305.891'401821—dc21
                          2003014792

1 2 3 4 5 08 07 06 05 04 03

Contents

v

Contents

Acknowledgements

This collection is the result of research conducted within the framework of the Programme for International Scientific Cooperation (PICS 740/CNRS): 'Locality, the Nation and the World from South Asia and Beyond: Critical Perspectives on "Globalisation" ', in collaboration with the Department of Anthropology of the London School of Economics and Political Science.

We express our thanks to the students, teachers and other contributors who participated from the United States, particularly Arjun Appadurai, David Brent, James Brown, Merry Burlingham, Partha Chatterjee, Vasudha Dalmia, Nick Dirks, Jennifer Eshelman, Wilhelm Halbfass, Bob Hardgrave, Ron Inden, Ward Keel, David Ludden, McKim Marriott, Sheldon Pollock, Elisabeth Povinelli, Gyan Prakash, Greg Possehl, Rosane Rocher, Marshall Sahlins, Sylvia Vatuk, Kamala Visweswaran, and Guy Welbon; as also to Chris Fuller, Sudipta Kaviraj, and Mrinalini Sinha in London, and Sanjay Subrahmanyam in Paris. We are grateful to David Phelps and James Walker for their linguistic contribution. Special thanks are also due to Rukun Advani, Rebecca Tolen, and Thomas Blom Hansen, as well as the two anonymous reviewers for their incisive comments on the Introduction.

A first collection of seven essays by Shahid Amin, Arjun Appadurai, Partha Chatterjee, Vasudha Dalmia, Sudipta Kaviraj, Gyan Prakash and Sanjay Subrahmanyam was published in a special issue of the journal *L'Homme*, 156 (2000). The collection also included reference articles providing a background to the essays. They were written by Jean-Loup Amselle, Jonathan Friedman, Jackie Assayag, Veronique Benei, and Jacques Pouchepadass. The collection was illustrated with colour reproductions of eight paintings by Shahzia Sikander, and introduced by Dana Self.

Paris, London, February 2003 J.A. & V.B.

Contributors

Shahid Amin is Professor of History at the University of Delhi.

Arjun Appadurai was until recently Samuel N. Harper Professor of Anthropology and of South Asian Languages and Civilizations at the University of Chicago. He is now at Yale University.

Jackie Assayag is Senior Research Fellow at the Centre National de la Recherche Scientifique, and a member of the Centre for Indian and South Asian Studies, Paris.

Véronique Bénéï is Research Fellow at the Centre National de la Recherche Scientifique and a member of Maison française d'Oxford; she is also Research fellow in Anthropology at the London School of Economics.

Urvashi Butalia is an independent writer and a publisher at Kali for Women, New Delhi.

Dipesh Chakrabarty is Professor of South Asian Studies and History at the University of Chicago.

Partha Chatterjee is Professor of Political Science at the Centre for Studies in Social Sciences, Calcutta; and Visiting Professor of Anthropology at Columbia University.

Contributors

Vasudha Dalmia is Professor of Hindi Literature and South Asian Studies at the University of California, Berkeley.

Prasenjit Duara is Professor of History and Chinese Studies at the University of Chicago.

Ramachandra Guha is an independent writer and visiting professor at several universities.

Akhil Gupta is Associate Professor of Cultural and Social Anthropology at Stanford University.

Sudipta Kaviraj is Professor of Political Science at the School of Oriental and African Studies, London.

Purnima Mankekar is Associate Professor of Cultural and Social Anthropology at Stanford University.

Gyan Prakash is Professor of History at Princeton University.

Sanjay Subrahmanyam is Directeur d'études (Research Professor) at the Ecole des Hautes Etudes en Sciences Sociales, Paris; and Professor of Indian History and Culture, Oxford University.

INTRODUCTION

At Home in Diaspora
South Asia, Europe, and America

JACKIE ASSAYAG
AND VÉRONIQUE BÉNÉÏ

'East is East and West is West, and never the twain shall meet . . .
But there is neither East nor West, Border, nor Breed, nor Birth,
When two strong men stand face to face, tho' they come from the
    ends of earth.

—Rudyard Kipling, *The Ballad of East and West* (1892)

Some dichotomies have enjoyed as great a vogue in academic circles as in popular wisdom: those between 'East' and 'West', between Europe and Asia or Africa, between 'the West' and 'the Rest'—'North' and 'South', as the current idiom currently has it. Yet our present insights, thanks to archaeologists,

1

epigraphists, philologists, historians, and (more recently) anthropologists, can no longer afford us any excuse for believing in the historical existence of any such cultural complexes that supposedly confront each other eye to eye without any admixture or intermingling, like separate islands in an archipelago. Not only has the 'frontier' between 'the West' and 'the Rest' of the world always been a shifting one, but the images and ideas, the practices and discourses that were encompassed by these labels have differed profoundly over time and from one country to another, from one society to another. They have depended on regional and national, social and cultural belonging, as well as on a variety of standpoints adopted here and there by merchants, travellers, missionaries, soldiers, administrators, settlers and the various different strata of indigenous societies.

There is no straightforward opposition between the so-called 'East' and 'West', but a hierarchical relation of multiple powers and modes of subordination that is more often than not a construct of Western ethnocentricity, inspired by the belief in a fundamental difference between distinct types of religions, races, humanities. Such differences have been linked to a geopolitical confrontation between unequally balanced powers that dates back long before the century of colonial conquest, and in which colonialism itself was a particular historical stage of development (and non-development). Contrary to Kipling's assertion, and that of so many others during the period of colonisation, 'East' and 'West' first met up with each other a very long time ago.

This is not to say that the world is an unbroken landscape. Our purpose is not to suggest that there has been a continual and undifferentiated intermingling of these cartographic imaginaries:

far from it. Varied scholars have sought to specify and demarcate with some precision the contours of these direct and indirect encounters between 'the West' and 'the non-West', and such a field of enquiry has now become a sizeable trend in the academe. Studies by François Hartog, Anthony Pagden, Nathan Wachtel, Serge Gruzinski, Tzvetan Todorov, Steven Greenblatt, Marshall Sahlins, Fred Cooper, Greg Dening, Tom Holt, Nick Thomas, Michel-Rolph Trouillot, Ann Stoler, to name but a few, offer rich and imaginative, interrelated and overlapping attempts at making sense of the process of interaction and appropriation, acculturation and hybridisation, collaboration and resistance which resulted from encounters that took place in almost every conceivable epoch and region. These approaches can be subsumed under three rubrics: those mostly interested in the issue of 'representation', images and cross-gazes that various cultures manufacture of one another across space and time, whether synchronically or diachronically; those that deal with 'contact', the twilight zone where dialogues and exchanges take place, and the ensuing multiple ways of accepting, misunderstanding and rejecting the Other. Lastly, those that address the issue of colonisation of imagination, body and mind, as well as of colonial cultures—material and non-material—in relation to the social fabric. These colonial cultures appear as specific producers of power and violence, the latter forces being at work in postcolonial societies even today, while assuming different forms through 'North–South' relations.

These three approaches are by no means mutually exclusive. Rather, they may overlap with one another and/or feed on each other. Work inspired by them has significantly contributed to documenting earlier multiple processes of 'globalisation'. As is well known, this kind of worldwide phenomenon is not a recent one:[1] there have been several waves of globalisation (as well as 'de-globalisation') in world history. From the sixteenth century on-wards, each of these has been accompanied by particular types of exchange and migration, accommodation, narration, negotiation and resistance.

Diaspora

Although exchanges and migrations from Asia to the Western world are old phenomena, these migratory flows of population have in the last two centuries been oriented towards the UK and the US, with an increasing preference towards the latter. Whereas in the earlier part of the twentieth century migration towards the US essentially originated from West European countries, at the close of the same century it predominantly concerned Asian and Latin American populations. In 1965 the law enforcing national immi-gration quotas was scrapped, and immigration from Asia and Latin America raised dramatically. The decade from 1990 to 2000 re-corded the highest wave of immigration in US history and the fast-est migratory rate in the world (a 57 per cent increase). According to the 2000 census, there were 31.1 million out of a total popula-tion of 281.4 million Americans who were born outside the US or whose parents were born outside the US.

Today, this migratory trend is intricately connected to the multifaceted process called 'globalisation', which encompasses geographical, economic, political, technological and cultural dimen-sions. The geographical expansion and ever greater density of inter-national trade, as well as the global networking of finance markets and the growing power of transnational corporations, have to be seen in relation to the ongoing 'revolution' of information and communications technology, as well as to the stream of images flowing from the culture industries. Such a politico-economic conjuncture has gone hand in hand with the reorganisation of the geo-political world order, to the effect that a more polycentric world and a 'postnational' politics have emerged in which transnational actors are growing in number and power alongside institutions. Concomitantly, however, the US has brought the question of national powers—with respect both to foreign and internal policy— back to the fore, particularly since the events of September 11th, 2001. At the same time, universal demands for human and minority rights and the principle of democracy have drawn unprecedented attention to the question of world poverty, the increasing circulation of populations, and the status of refugees.

The definitive asymmetries of power and the structural relationship between the 'West' and the so-called 'Third World' were first characterised in the social sciences by the dominance of discourses on modernisation and development that marked the period after decolonisation. These discourses began to decline with the advent of critical approaches of both Third-worldism (or 'critical Fanonism') and ethnocentric views of world history. Supporting such approaches were identity claims made by minority communities, the debate about orientalism, and the development of cultural studies. All of these critiques were instrumental in the crisis of representation that has since then taken place in the social sciences.[2] In the last decade, however, the emphasis has shifted from the languages and life-worlds of the disenfranchised, subaltern consciousness, and 'postorientalism' to new topics and 'objects' of inquiry, underscoring the agency of the social actors of 'postcoloniality' and 'multiple' or 'alternative modernities'.

As mentioned above, such a reconfiguration of the field of social sciences has been accompanied by a change in the structure of research and academic institutions in the Western academy, more so in the American than the British: these institutions have become more internationalised and have included 'Third World' scholars. All these trends and reconfigurations have constituted the postcolonial scholar's presence in 'the West' as a phenomenon worthy of analysis. In particular, they have raised the question of the impact of these scholars' work on research both on the 'West' and the 'non-West'. So far, this impact has involved comparatively little research in relation to South Asian scholars.

'Asian Indians' represent only the third largest sub-group within the 'Asian' category (1.9 million out of 11.9 million), and account for a mere 0.67 per cent of the total US population (barely 16 per cent of the 'Asian' population). Yet their position stands out as a particularly successful one. Of all immigrants—and in comparison with earlier waves of immigration—South Asians in the US are often presented, somewhat stereotypically, as embodying the quintessential late twentieth century late-capitalist migration 'success story' (Helweg and Helweg 1990). This diaspora[3] represents the movement of a largely middle class, fairly well educated, English-speaking professional population, all criteria which have contributed to the longstanding popular image of South Asians as 'good immigrants' or a 'model minority'. Moreover, South Asians have long occupied a distinctive position, mediating between Black and White populations.[4] According to Vijay Prashad (2000), their 'love of fair skin', 'admiration of high spirituality' and 'deep attachment to their (Aryan) nation (*desh*)' even make South Asians an easy weapon for the racist White American community to use against Blacks. In any case, the South Asian diaspora is well integrated today and has become markedly more visible in popular culture in the past decade, from the *New York Times* bestselling fiction list to films, television sitcoms, and fashions in food. It is also present in many economic niches, from taxi drivers, news vendors, to engineers, physicians and IT technicians.

The writers of most of the present essays occupy positions of privilege in their working lives—that is, by American standards. In this sense, although they may be perceived as representing the voice of most other migrants, they are representative neither of those who are also supposedly globalised yet much less secure in their positions as nomads, nor of the millions of South Asians who are too poor to leave the soil on which they have been toiling for generations. The position of the present contributors thus illustrates the inequality of displacement found in many instances of migration, whereby access to global mobility often reflects and further reinforces social stratification and inequality both within and beyond national boundaries.

'Native' social scientists have—at least in Anglophone countries—been incorporated into the Western academic world since the 1950s.[5] Yet this was first in a subordinate position—as regional specialists, i.e. as part of 'area studies' and foreign (i.e. non-European) language-teaching programmes (cf. Jackie Assayag 2000). Notwithstanding the notable exceptions in the 1950s of the Mysore anthropologist M.N. Srinivas at Oxford, or, later, the historian Tapan Raychaudhuri likewise at Oxford—a history of circulation briefly retraced in this volume by Sanjay Subrahmanyam—

it is only in the last twenty-five years that a group of South Asian intellectuals has been successful in transcending such a closely-knit order.[6] In keeping with a general trend whereby scholars of non-Western origin now occupy a range of high-profile positions in the academic field, a growing number of teaching and research posts in South Asian studies are now held by academics of South Asian origin, especially in the US and UK, as well as (although more recently, and in lesser numbers) in Germany, Northern Europe and Australia. Most such scholars have settled in these countries over the last twenty years or so.

Diasporic Intellectuals in the Academy

That Europe has long developed research traditions and produced much scholarly work on Asia often tends to obscure the prior existence of knowledge traditions in Indian, Chinese and Japanese civilisations. Yet, in spite of those existing traditions, it is only in the last three decades that an increased production of knowledge has emerged from studies conducted by Asian scholars 'at home', arguably challenging past research trends and contributing to a renewed vision of these societies and cultures. Their impact has, however, been very little analysed. By increasingly holding academic positions in the most prestigious institutions in 'the West', have these Asian scholars helped to redefine the canon and reconsider the links between disciplines (i.e. anthropology and history)? By developing what were considered 'new questions' and 'new approaches', have they helped to evolve 'new paradigms' or a new 'regime of knowledge' for research, thus contributing to pathbreaking research in social sciences? These questions have so far attracted scant attention from the academic community as a whole. Nor has the voice of scholars of South Asian descent been much heard on the matter.

In order to address these questions 'from within' and to provide an account of the transformations occurring in South Asian studies across Europe, India and the United States, the editors of the present volume invited social scientists of South Asian origin to contribute to this 'dossier' (a shorter version of this was first published in the French anthropological journal *L'Homme*).[7] Each scholar was requested to write a short reflexive account of their personal and academic experience in (relation to) the 'West', together with their reflections on transformations of knowledge about Asia. In particular, they were invited to discuss whether their presence or that of other South Asian colleagues in the 'West' has significantly influenced the development of the social sciences, and whether South Asian scholars studying South Asia have produced an identifiable body of scholarship that explicitly marks their collective endeavours. It is hoped that this reflexive exercise will help address at least two connected questions (which can also be approached along the axes of sociological works addressing the institutional location of the postcolonial *homo academicus* more explicitly): why should such a development happen at this point in history, between the 1960s and the 1990s? How have the writers' work, thought and lives been shaped by the encounter with different area studies and multiple modernities?

Although the present collection is devoted to some members of this intellectual diaspora and their 'travelling theories', to provide a full picture of the wide world of diasporic intellectuals or South Asian scholars is far beyond the scope of this book, if only because, far from forming a cohesive 'school', there are discordant voices among them (here, notably those of Ramachandra Guha and Sanjay Subrahmanyam). The aim of this book is, more modestly, to locate readings of South Asian personal narratives in relation to India and 'the West' in a historical and sociological context. A set of four different and complementary remarks need to be made at this stage.

First, our purpose is not to formulate a critique or to assess the respective merits of South Asian scholars' contributions; rather, it is to inform academic discussions and intellectual histories that surround it. Second, this volume is to be distinguished from others (for example Chaturvedi 2000; Ludden 2001) that have sought to restrict their investigation to the intellectual debates generated by the work of the Subaltern Studies collective. Unlike those, this book focuses on the links between intellectual autobiography and scholarly production while paying heed to the scholars' affective and cognitive experience of 'travelling cultures'. In short, this volume is made up of stories of scholarly trajectories as well as the connected histories of both scholars and theories travelling across countries, national academies, and intellectual landscapes. By attempting to make sense of the complexity and variation of the relations that obtain among individuals and between bodies of knowledge in different locations, it affords us an opportunity to underscore the importance that is currently being invested in individual and collective migrations and biographies (see Appadurai, this volume) in the circulation of lived experiences and acquisition of knowledge across vast geographic distances. It also allows us to recall that, although the situation of the migrant does create a sense of identity, such an identity is renegotiated from time to time in relation to the regional or national contexts within which it operates.

Third, the collection presented here does not exhort us to 'get inside the heads' of 'natives', nor to read over their shoulders, nor to reconstruct what they thought (as some anthropologists would have it). It proposes only, and much more pressingly, that we should read these texts, or at least the majority of them, as the products of scholars living 'at home in diaspora'. These Indian academics are invited to visit universities across the world. All have been partly educated on the subcontinent. Some have diplomas from European and North American institutions and hold a professorial chair on the subcontinent, or in Europe or the United States, or sometimes in both places at once: in short, they are 'transnational' or 'translocated', 'globalised' or 'hybrid' intellectuals—to use some recent items of jargon. The present essays afford us a chance to hear what these intellectuals have to say on what is both an object and an area of study, South Asia, which happens to be, or to have been, the environment in which they lived, worked, and conducted their research. Its social fabric is native to them and known from the inside, with the familiarity that springs from *habitus* and *conatus*, to say nothing of the linguistic competence arguably acquired alongside.[8] Such closeness to one's object of study may also elicit emotions—such as passion and nostalgia—and entertain illusions caused by or arising in spite of the fact of exile. For example, such emotions and illusions may blur the distinction between scholars' political self-affirmation and the critique of the Eurocentric character of 'Indian studies' as practised since the eighteenth century—from then on labelled 'Orientalism'.[9] The postcolonial or subaltern scholar's visibility in metropolitan institutions of higher education has therefore led to the charge of the empire 'writing back', enabled by the various brands of identity politics and multiculturalism that have hyper-politicised academic institutions, especially in the US.

Yet, and lastly, this collection of essays is not based on the fallacious notion that the voice of the 'native' carries greater authority—being the vehicle of who knows what 'native truth'—by virtue of its autochthony or indigenous character: a set of ideas that Marshall Sahlins rightly taunts as 'pidgin anthropology' and 'pop nativism'. At no point in the stages of its preparation has this volume sought to serve as the vehicle for an ethnic claim, or to defend a cultural or multicultural orientation in the field of social studies. In the process, however, the editors are aware of possibly having contributed to the construction of a record and a memory—or even a hagiography?—of the South Asian academic diaspora, especially since most of the contributors (Shahid Amin, Arjun Appadurai, Urvashi Butalia, Partha Chatterjee, Vasudha Dalmia, Akhil Gupta, Purnima Mankekar) have chosen to commit themselves to the genre of autobiography.

Be that as it may, we are convinced that, along with the enterprise of objectifying sociology via working on statistical data—an enterprise whose potential we have no intention of denying—there is room for a series of essays in ego-history.[10] The reader may want to read these scholars as much for who they are as for what they represent. Their essays will be of value as documentation even though—or because—they are based on the minutiae of individual human existence. And that is not just because all theory is partly biographical, but equally because the investment that these lives embody escapes the anonymity of the detached observer, the customs posts of specific academic disciplines, and of all 'Western' enclosure. Far from taking us away from research, these testimonies bring us back to it through an understanding made possible by an appreciation of much wider horizons.

Decolonising the Imagination of the Social Sciences

Today, not only have 'Other' cultures ceased to be confined to other parts of the world with the overcoming of spatial and temporal distances inherent in technological globalisation, but human diversity and cultural differences have taken on new significance. Historians, whether Euro-Americans or others, are studying regional interconnectednesses within the same world history. In other words, social scientists now put themselves in the same frame of reference as their objects of study. At the same time, the boundaries of the social sciences have been redefined both by the political engagement of social groups that had for a long time been merely 'observed', and equally by the wider social spread of information (magazines, films, newspapers) as well as the intervention of international organisations (Survival International, NGOs, the UNO, the IMF, the World Bank) (Bénéï 1998). Better still, the 'Others' are now playing a crucial part in setting distant cultures in relation to each other, within a framework that is more critical and heuristic. So, the geopolitics of the relations between 'East' and 'West' have been radically redrawn.

This collection thus takes as its vantage point the testimony and reflections of researchers whose status was initially determined by their coming from zones of dependence or so-called 'periphery', 'underdeveloped', 'less developed' or 'developing' countries. Their peoples were long deemed unworthy of a history, or even an 'ethnohistory', the prefix 'ethno-' serving generally to degrade and to belittle the disciplines and bodies of knowledge so qualified—as if colonisation had not, to paraphrase Frantz Fanon, reached completion with the departure of the last white policeman and the final handover ceremony. Such past disparaging terminology has sustained the vivid feeling—despite the universal recognition among South Asian scholars—of them being 'subaltern[ist]'.

As it happens, most of the contributors here have been deeply influenced by a subaltern/ist perspective. As is well known, this approach was initially aimed at bringing the autonomy of subaltern consciousness into light by producing a historiography 'from below', that is, freed from colonialist and nationalist influence (Pouchepadass 2000). The objective was to rip apart the veils of power which had shrouded peasant and popular—and more recently women's—resistance in the rhetoric of codification, whether orientalist, colonial or nationalist. A series of questions cuts across the writings of subalternist historians: can other modes of relation be imagined between history, society and culture? Are the historiographic models of scholars from decolonised countries specific? Who speaks for the Indian past (and 'the non-West')? Can the reflection on historical writing in a postcolonial context provide the historical discipline with new approaches, namely through disputing the historiographical model which has been elaborated in Europe since the Enlightenment? In other words, what are the possible ways of 'provincialising Europe' and what does it mean to be a 'Barbarian' today, to use the programmatic book title coined by

14

Dipesh Chakrabarty, and the ironic expression which Sudipta Kaviraj claims for himself, respectively (both in this volume).

These questions are central to most of the contributors' concerns. Some devote themselves particularly to historicising the process of their intellectual formation (whether in India—the Naxalbari rebellion in north-eastern Bengal; the US—Civil Rights movement, opposition to the Vietnam war; or in Europe—the 1968 student protests); others pay greater attention to the relationship between politicised intellectual formation and narrative form. Thus the political question of relating theoretical Marxism to the problems of transition in colonial societies, the student politics of the radical left in the 1970s, and the pernicious and stultifying effects of a state-sponsored brand of anti-colonial nationalism, all form a significant narrative arc in the essays by Shahid Amin, Dipesh Chakrabarty, Prasenjit Duara, and Gyan Prakash.

Area studies and anthropology (in the 1960s and 1970s) were also important formative influences on these scholars. The cognitive construction of South Asia was institutionalised in the American university system by means of area studies programmes (which were the result of geo-political strategies and often owed more to American foreign affairs policy than to 'mere' academic objectives). The arrival of large numbers of South-Asian-American students over the past two decades has created a new demand for area studies courses, and this kind of faculty position (see Bénéï 2000). Furthermore, many of the historians and researchers in political science owe a great part of their reputation to an approach inspired by anthropology, the kind they discovered and appropriated to themselves in the shape of the 'cultural' variety 'made in the USA'.

15

The innovative character of the researches of authors of South Asian origin is indubitably linked to the diffusion of this cultural anthropology throughout various disciplines, whether in the field of the humanities or of the social sciences. Conversely, the renewed resilience of this kind of anthropology resides in its capacity to sunder walls, go beyond area studies, and guarantee the circulation of ideas as well as cross older boundaries and explore new horizons.

Doing away with old barriers has not, however, dispensed with the question of representation, particularly with respect to matters of contemporary import. From the relations between religion, politics and nationality to those between myth and history and between democratic government and secularism—to say nothing of those pertaining to the Vedic tradition, Orientalism, colonialism, communalism, Christianity and Islam, often with reference to the rise to power of the jingoistic ideology of Hindutva[11]—the question of 'who speaks for whom?' has remained salient. Although these debates about issues of representation reflect a long-standing and rich intellectual tradition in the subcontinent, they have not exhausted it. For instance, can a South Asian intellectual speak for anyone except his/her own class, gender, community, region, nationality? More generally, can anyone else speak for another's class, gender, community, religion, nationality?

Above all, if this collection invites us to listen and pay heed to 'an otherness'—one that is modulated by varying tones—it is because some of the contributors propose for examination a critique that would see itself as both radical and fundamental. Radical in regard to the regimes of discourse of foreign observers of non-Western cultures—not only Indian, but also Chinese (Prasenjit Duara). Fundamental with regard to the specific situations that have made possible the sum total of these discursive expressions. In both cases the ambition held by some of them of re-establishing social science research on new foundations comes to light (Gyan Prakash).[12] Against the universalist, rationalist and individualist blindness of the intellectuals of the 1950s and 1960s, which allegedly fostered a worldview anchored in no specific vantage point, their project is 'defined' *stricto sensu* by the idea of localisation: any knowledge, like the men and women that create it, must be 'sited'/ 'situated' (Shahid Amin). In sum, there could not be any discipline, any organisation of knowledge, any institution or epistemology, autonomous in respect of the socio-cultural, historical and political formations that have fashioned the idiosyncracies of a specific period or place (Dipesh Chakrabarty).

Such an approach pertains to an 'era of suspicion' tracing its direct descent to the debates on the politics and culture of 'difference and identity' in the world, and more precisely in the United States. There, the politics and culture of 'difference and identity' have been shaped in part by conflicts over the issues of ethnicity, racism and antiracism ('colour-blind ideologies') and those of gender, feminism and women's rights (addressed here by Urvashi Butalia and Purnima Mankekar). These debates and questions have been undergirded by a historicist epistemology, as applied to the 'hard sciences' by Thomas S. Kuhn and to the social sciences by Foucault (cf. his 'archaeology' and 'genealogy' articulated around the concepts of 'knowledge' and 'power'—a method labelled 'poststructuralism' in the US).[13] Associated with such a historicist epistemology, the congruence between the conceptual framework of Edward Said and the 'linguistic turn' has also been an illuminating one.[14]

Let us emphasise that the categorical imperative of 'localisation' leads us to take into reckoning the position that all interpreters of cultures currently occupy in the academic field, as much in 'the West' as in 'the East'. This, in all fairness, entails turning back the questions of the 'location of scholarship' (Gyan Prakash), and of speaking on behalf of others (Sanjay Subrahmanyam), on the authors of this collection themselves. Such a reversal of questions is nothing new and has generated considerable debate, both within the circles of 'localised scholars' and outside. It is not our purpose to assess their arguments. More simply, readers who are interested may refer to the work of the many academics who have sought to render explicit the criticisms that it is possible to level against them.[15]

Briefly, these criticisms range from a way of resisting European hegemony that is none the less expressed in European concepts and terminology (Sahlins)[16] to an élitist endeavour to fit oneself up with a transdisciplinary niche within the Anglophone academic system (Ahmad 1991, 1995; Robbins 1993: Chapters 5 and 6); a *comprador* bourgeoisie of Western style and educational background, composed of a group of intellectuals who play a mediating role in trading the cultural merchandise of global capitalism in and for the periphery (Appiah 1991: 149); a legitimation, on the academic stage of 'globalisation', of globalised thinkers (Friedman 1999); a means of specifying a discomfort and a conflict in political terms, if not merely a way of serving as a moral guarantor of American imperialism (Dirlik 1997, Chapter 3); an obscurantist enterprise that serves as 'a psychic framework for counter-revolutions' (Chomsky 1998); a claim by affluent émigrés purporting to speak for the voiceless victims attached to a particular locality (Bauman 1998, Chapter 4); a response to the shame felt by the Indian élite at having collaborated with the British colonisers (Marriott);[17] and an anti-modern neo-traditionalism feeding on a vague nostalgia for authentic communities (Sarkar 1997, 1999). In short, such criticisms boil down to an accusation of proffering a culturalist, theoreticist, identitarian, differentialist diversion in the field of the social sciences.

Localisation and Knowledge

To sum up, this collection's heuristic ambition is fourfold: it is to deal with issues connecting with the publishing scene, with institutions, with the politics of knowledge, as well as with epistemology. First, despite the mainstream of English-speaking academic publications favouring all those whom Sahlins calls the 'afterologues'[18] and the other 'post-everythings' (postmodernists, poststructuralists, postcolonialists, etc.), it is still not certain that it is their representatives who currently hold posts with decision-power in the academic field—especially in the US. This field appears in the last analysis largely impenetrable to any radical calling into question of received ideas. However, and secondly, the integration of researchers from the so-called 'Third World' into the research institutions of the so-called 'First World', operating on the same level as Westerners in the learned community, reconfigures the international academic division of labour. This it does by progressively dissolving the question of otherness between 'them' and 'us', that differential ontology which fostered Orientalism and with which anthropology and history conflated themselves while aiming at understanding others ('how do we think they think?'). Thirdly, the intervention of these new interlocutors in the public space broadens the discussion and re-deals the playing cards of controversy on matters of colonialism and imperialism; local and global capitalism; and questions bearing upon national traditions, whether in the academic or in the most banal patriotic or hegemonic sense. All these are questions raised both by the issue of non-European worlds entering into the arena of modernity and by the social making of multiple modernities.

Finally, and more generally, the epistemological regime (sometimes qualified as non-Popperian) of the so-called social 'sciences' requires an exploration of the places and enunciatory modes in which theories are propounded, just as much as the clarification of the 'conditions of production' of all such theories, including those that glorify '(de)localisation'. This is a necessary prolegomenon to any discipline with any pretense to rigour, coherence, or consistency—but one that has to be undertaken after taking good care not to confuse the conditions of its enunciation with the truth-value of its propositions, or the validity of its reasoning. Indeed, one can admit that the principle of value neutrality is a biased one. But it would be contradictory for an intellectual to reduce theories only to their localisation, precisely because they aim at a certain generality: that is what makes them theories, after all. Even if the diasporic thinkers proffering these theories have largely contributed to redefining a large part of the various fields and disciplines of the social sciences and beyond—to the point of sometimes blurring the distinction between the scholar, the moralist and the politician—

the sociology of 'localisation' exhausts neither the field of knowledge as a whole nor the debate on norms of rationality.

NOTES

1. On illusions about the 'newness' of globalisation, see Sidney W. Mintz (1998); cf. also Jackie Assayag (1998) for a critical approach to globalisation as conceptualised by Arjun Appadurai (1996).

2. It is noteworthy that the recent trend of postcolonial and subalternist critique has endorsed the early-twentieth-century Western traditions of critical Marxism (Gramsci) as well as the philosophical critique of the violence of Enlightenment Reason (Adorno, Horkheimer) and, to a lesser extent, the sociological one of Euro-American modernity (Chicago school, Riesman).

3. For the semantic problems posed today by the use of this notion, originally exclusively used of the diaspora of the Jews, see James Clifford (1997: Chapter 10).

4. That they are seen as White in the US is an important difference between the US and the UK in understandings of both race relations and historical connections of immigrants to the old empire.

5. For Britain, see Bénéï (2000); for the United States, see Assayag (2000) and Dirks (forthcoming).

6. Cf. Srinivas's own reflections (Srinivas 1966; Srinivas, Shah and Ramaswamy (eds) 1979). The autobiographical comments of Raychaudhuri can be read in the preface to his most recent work (Raychaudhuri 1999). Cf. also Chang, Mankekar and Gupta (2002) for an early autobiographical account of the South Asian experience in America of the man of letters Dhan Gopal Mukerji (1890–1936). Cf. also Narayan (1993) and Ohnuki-Tierney (1984) for more recent accounts of native anthropologists in America.

7. Among the authors contacted, some expressed an unwillingness to take part in this exercise for various reasons, usually couched in the form of

21

'I would prefer not to . . .', to borrow the expression immortalised in Herman Melville's novel *Bartleby*.

8. On the privileged position occupied by the academic sharing his/her informant's mother tongue in fieldwork situation, cf. Sudipta Kaviraj (1992).

9. Such a critique is itself heir to the anti-imperialist critique of the social science programme of area studies which saw its rise to power at the University of California, Berkeley, during the 1960s. Edward Said (1978) gives examples of the latter dubious interaction between specialised area studies and the decision-making process of the American government, as much in internal as in external policy.

10. See for instance the essays by French historians assembled by Pierre Nora (1987).

11. Here the testimony of the Sanskritist Wendy Doniger (1999: 944) is of value: 'We who had once studied the *Rig Veda* with awe in small classes consisting of a mix of passionately devoted ex-hippies and coldly brilliant linguists came to react to the word "Veda" as if someone had said "fascism" (more precisely "right-wing militant Hinduism").'

12. In the field of Indian studies, cf. the reflections of Dipesh Chakrabarty (1992; 1995) and the polemical exchanges between the 'subalternist' Gyan Prakash (1990, 1992) and representatives of the so-called 'Cambridge School', Rosalind O'Hanlon and David Washbrook (1992); that between Carol Breckenridge and Peter van der Veer (1993) on the one hand, and, on the other, Wilhelm Halbfass (Preisendanz and Preisendanz 1997); and lastly, those between David Washbrook (1997, 1998, 1999) and Peter van der Veer (1998, 1999).

13. An interesting article by David A. Hollinger (1997) details and comments on the progress of these debates in the United States. On the drift of the American academic left, cf. the work of Richard Rorty (1998).

14. Let us recall that the book *Orientalism* (1978) only concerns the Middle East; for a reflection on South Asia taking its point of departure from the work of Edward Said, cf. Carol A. Breckenridge and Peter van der Veer (1993).

15. See *Public Culture*, vol. 6(1), 1993 for a dossier presenting various viewpoints on these controversies.
16. Interview with Marshall Sahlins, Chicago, October 7, 1999.
17. Interview with McKim Marriott, Chicago, October 7, 1999.
18. Sahlins (1996: 423, 1999: 404, 416) recalls that the term 'afterological studies' was coined by Jaqueline Mraz.

REFERENCES

Ahmad, Aijaz. 1991. 'Between Orientalism and Historicism: Anthropological Knowledge of India'. *Studies in History* 7(1): 135–63.

———. 1995. 'The Politics of Literary Postcoloniality', *Race and Class*, 36 (3): 1–20.

Amselle, Jean-Loup. 2000. 'La globalisation. "Grand partage" ou mauvais cadrage?'. *L'Homme* 156: 207–26.

Appadurai, Arjun. 1996. *Modernity at Large. Cultural Dimensions of Globalization*. Minneapolis-London, University of Minnesota Press.

Appiah, Anthony. 1991. 'Is the Post- in Postmodernism the Post- in Postcolonialism?'. *Critical Enquiry*, 17: 336–57.

Assayag, Jackie. 1998. 'La culture comme fait social global? Anthropologie et (post)modernité'. *L'Homme* 148: 201–24.

———. 2000. 'L'Asie du Sud "made in the USA": Transferts culturels, institutions universitaires, et diaspora intellectuelle'. *L'Homme*, 156: 99–130.

——— and Véronique Bénéï. Eds. 2000. *Intellectuels en diaspora et théories nomades. L'Homme*, 156, October.

Bauman, Zygmunt. 1998. *Globalization. The Human Consequences*. London, Polity Press and Blackwell.

Bénéï, Véronique. 1998. 'Régime de scientificité ou "régime de vulgarisation"?'. *Gradhiva* 23: 127–33.

———. 2000. 'Nations, diaspora et *area studies*: l'Asie du Sud, de la Grande-Bretagne aux États-Unis'. *L'Homme* 156, October: 131–60.

Breckenridge, Carol A. and Peter van der Veer. Eds. 1993. *Orientalism and the Postcolonial Predicament. Perpectives on South Asia*. Philadelphia, University of Pennsylvania Press.

Chakrabarty, Dipesh. 1992. 'Postcoloniality and the Artifice of History: Who Speaks for the Indian Past?'. *Representations* 37: 1–26.

———. 1995. 'Radical Histories and the Question of Enlightenment Rationalism: Some Recent Critics of Subaltern Studies'. *Economic and Political Weekly*. 751–9.

Chang, Gordon H., Purnima Mankekar and Akhil Gupta. Eds. 2002. *Caste and Outcast. Dhan Gopal Mukerji*. Stanford, Stanford University Press.

Chaturvedi, Vinayak. Ed. 2000. *Mapping Subaltern Studies and the Postcolonial*. London, Verso.

Chomsky, Noam. 1998. 'Le vrai visage de la critique postmoderniste'. *Agone* 18–19: 49–62.

Dirlik, Arif. 1997. *The Postcolonial Aura. Third World Criticism in the Age of Global Capitalism*. Boulder, CO, Westview Press.

Dirks, Nicholas B. Forthcoming. 'South Asian Studies: Futures Past'. In David Szanton. Ed. *The Politics of Knowledge: Area Studies and the Discipline*. Chapter 9. California International and Area Studies.

Doniger, Wendy. 1999. 'Presidential Address: "I have Scinde": Flogging a Dead (White Male Orientalist) Horse'. *Journal of Asian Studies* 58 (4): 940–60.

Fahim, Hussain and Katherine Helmer. Eds. 1980. 'Indigenous Anthropology in Non-Western Countries: A Further Elaboration'. *Current Anthropology* 21 (5): 644–62.

Friedman, Jonathan. 1999. 'The Hybridisation of the Roots and the Abhorrence of the Bush'. In Mike Featherstone and Scott Lash. Eds. *Space and Culture. City, Nation, World*. London, Thousand Oaks-New Delhi, Sage Publications Ltd: 230–56.

———. 2000. 'Des racines et (dé)routes. Tropes pour trekkers'. *L'Homme* 156: 187–206.

Halbfass, Wilhelm. 1988. *India and Europe. An Essay in Understanding*. Albany, State University of New York Press.

Helweg, Arthur W. and Usha M. Helweg. 1990. *An Immigrant Success Story: East Indians in America*. London, Hurst & Co.

Hollinger, David A. 1997. 'The Disciplines and the Identity Debates, 1970–1995'. *Daedalus* 126 (1): 333–51.

Kaviraj, Sudipta. 1992. 'Writing, Speaking, Being: Language and the Historical Formation of Identities in India'. In D. Hellman-Rajanayagam and D. Rothermund. Eds. *Nationalstaat und Sprachkonflikte in Süd- und Südostasien*. Stuttgart, Franz Steiner Verlag.

Ludden, David. Ed. 2001. *Reading Subaltern Studies. Critical History, Contested Meaning, and the Globalization of South Asia*. Delhi, Permanent Black.

Mintz, Sidney, W. 1998. 'The Localisation of Anthropological Practice. From Area Studies to Transnationalism'. *Critique of Anthropology* 18 (2): 117–33.

Narayan, Kirin. 1993. 'How Native is a 'Native' Anthropologist?'. *American Anthropologist* 95 (3): 671–86.

Nora, Pierre. 1987. *Essais d'Ego-histoire. Maurice Agulhon, Pierre Chaunu, Georges Duby, Raoul Girardet, Jacques Le Goff, Michelle Perrot, René Raymond*. Paris, Gallimard.

O'Hanlon, Rosalind and David Washbrook. 1992. 'After Orientalism: Culture, Criticism, and Politics in the Third World'. *Comparative Studies in Society and History* 34 (1): 141–67.

Ohnuki-Tierney, Emiko. 1984. ' "Native" Anthropologists'. *American Ethnologist* 11 (3): 584–6.

Pouchepadass, Jacques. 2000. 'Les *Subaltern Studies* ou la critique postcoloniale de la modernité'. *L'Homme* 156: 161–86.

Prakash, Gyan. 1990. 'Writing Post-Orientalist Histories of the Third World: Perpectives from Indian Historiography'. *Comparative Studies in Society and History* 32 (2): 383–408.

———. 1992. 'Can the Subaltern Ride? A Reply to O'Hanlon and Washbrook'. *Comparative Studies in Society and History* 34 (1): 168–84.

Prashad, Vijay. 2000. *Karma of Brown Folk*. Minneapolis, University of Minnesota Press.

Franco, Eli, and Karin Preisendanz. Eds. 1997. *Beyond Orientalism. The World of Wilhelm Halbfass and its Impact on India and Cross-cultural Studies.* Amsterdam/Atlanta, Rodolphi.

Raychaudhuri, Tapan. 1999. *Perceptions, Emotions, Sensibilities. Essays on India's Colonial and Post-colonial Experiences.* Delhi, Oxford University Press.

Robbins, Brice. 1993. *Secular Vocations. Intellectuals, Professionalism, Culture.* London, Verso.

Rorty, Richard. 1998. *Achieving Our Country.* Cambridge, MA, Harvard University Press ('Leftist Thought in Twentieth-Century-America').

Sahlins, Marshall. 1996. 'The Sadness of Sweetness. The Native Anthropology of Western Cosmology'. *Current Anthropology* 37 (3): 395–428.

———. 1999. 'Two or Three Things that I Know about Culture'. *The Journal of the Royal Anthropological Institute* 5 (3): 399–421.

Said, Edward W. 1978. *Orientalism.* New York, Pantheon Books.

———. 1989. 'Representing the Colonized: Anthropology's Interlocutors'. *Critical Inquiry* 15: 205–25.

Sarkar, Sumit. 1997. 'The Decline of the Subaltern in *Subaltern Studies*'. In Sumit Sarkar, *Writing Social History.* Delhi, Oxford University Press: 83–108.

———. 1999. 'Postmodernism and the Writing of History'. *Studies in History* 15 (2): 293–322.

Srinivas, Mysore Narasimhachar. 1966. 'Some Thoughts on the Study of One's Own Society'. In M.N. Srinivas. Ed. *Social Change in Modern India.* Berkeley, University of California Press: 147–63.

———, A.M. Shah and E.A. Ramaswamy. Eds. 1979. *The Fieldworker and the Field. Problems and Challenge in Sociological Investigation.* Delhi, Oxford University Press.

Van der Veer, Peter. 1998. 'The Global History of Modernity'. *Journal of the Economic and Social History of the Orient* 41(3): 285–94.

———. 1999. 'All that is Solid Melts into Thin Air'. *Journal of the Economic and Social History of the Orient* 42 (4): 566–8.

Washbrook, David. 1997. 'From Comparative Sociology to Global History: Britain and India in the Pre-History of Modernity'. *Journal of the Economic and Social History of the Orient* 40 (4): 410–43.

————. 1998. 'The Global History of 'Modernity'—A Response to a Reply'. *Journal of the Economic and Social History of the Orient* 41 (3): 295–311.

————. 1999. '. . . And Having Melted into Thin Air, then Rains Down Again'. *Journal of the Economic and Social History of the Orient* 42 (4): 569–74.

1

Knowledge, Circulation and Collective Biography

ARJUN APPADURAI

I t has become obvious that some intellectuals from South
Asia (and from the East more generally) are speaking in the
West, to the West, and about the West (as well as the East). It
has also become a new form of tendentious criticism to reduce
these persons, who include me, to being self-interested voices of
their privileged double positions. Thus, even for those who are
reticent about bringing their stories into their theories, it seems a
good moment to recognise that the view from nowhere (always an
arrogant fiction in one sort of Western epistemology) comes partly

from a new kind of somewhere. Reflections on how my own intellectual biography is linked up with some others like mine, is one way to do this. So the little essay that follows is offered as a collective, and interactive, biography—a kind of prosopography.

Some facts: I arrived in the United States in 1967, already part of the first generation of young Indians who had become sceptical of the dominant fetish of science and technology as male careers, and of the fading glamour of Oxford and Cambridge for young postcolonials. My first stop in the United States, Brandeis University, was a deeply counter-cultural institution created by wealthy American Jews to provide a safe haven for bright Jewish students kept out of the Ivy League and for brilliant European intellectuals displaced by Hitler. My financial benefactor was Lawrence Wien, who founded a scholarship programme at Brandeis strictly for foreign students, and placed no restrictions whatsoever on what we studied and how long we took to get the BA. The late 1960s were a time when students and faculty at Brandeis and elsewhere were saturated with the euphoria of social criticism (a potent mixture of Marx and Freud patented by Herbert Marcuse, who had just left Brandeis for San Diego) and the sense of a progressive social contract between Blacks, Jews, socialists, students and everyone opposed to the Vietnam war. The assassinations of Robert Kennedy and Martin Luther King in 1968 focused this energy and created an exuberant political hedonism. Brandeis also gave me my first exposure to the history of ideas (with Alasdair Macintyre), to sociology (with Kurt Wolff and Lewis Coser, both products of Simmelian social theory with its neo-Kantian roots), and to a host of more modest theoretical waves, such as Maslow's theories of self-actualisation. This was a moral brand of social science, leavened by the humanities, innocent of training, method or doctrine, thick with the aroma of dissent.

Even at this stage I had a serious interest in research on some aspect of modern India. This was hard to nurture at Brandeis, where the focus was on the liberal arts, experimental social science, and undergraduate interests. But I was able to locate some teachers with an interest in India, who gave me the opportunity to do some serious reading in what I later understood to be area studies. At this stage, I explored the social and intellectual history of India in the nineteenth century and began to discover the ways in which India, and the developing world more generally, was seen in the United States through the lens of modernisation theory and various debates about development. It was at Brandeis that I first developed a sense of the rich literature on South Asia and the complex ways in which social science, the humanities, and the history of the British Empire had produced a huge archive of the South Asian world. I did not quite know that I had embarked on a life-long engagement with what in the United States was already called area studies. In retrospect, I see this as the thread of continuity in my scholarly life from 1967 until the present, and so I shall remark on its changing appearances in my career throughout this essay.

With a BA nominally in history, and a very good record (no amount of mind-numbing music and counter-cultural bacchanalia could inhibit the conditioning of a Tamil Brahmin male from a bourgeois Indian background), I did well enough to get a scholarship to the University of Chicago. The scholarship was to admit me to the Committee on Social Thought (now perhaps better known as the home of Saul Bellow and Allan Bloom, for those who follow the gossipy side of American literary criticism). Part of my financial support came from the Committee on Southern Asian Studies, a body that brought together (and still does) resources for the study of South Asia across the University of Chicago. So, at least from 1970, when I arrived in Chicago, I was destined to study social science in a humanistic milieu, with area studies as my anchor. That much has not changed in the three decades since.

The University of Chicago was a heady place in the early 1970s for someone with my interests. Hannah Arendt and Harold Rosenberg came regularly to teach in the Committee on Social Thought from their regular positions in New York. I studied Machiavelli's *The Prince* with Arendt and Dostoyevsky's *The Brothers Karamazov* with Harold Rosenberg, as part of the monastic 'great books' curriculum that defined this extraordinary academic department. It included classicists, Shakespeare scholars, artists, novelists, sociologists and critics. When I was doing my graduate work the faculty included the fearsome and bitter Edward Shils, the coldly patrician Saul Bellow, the Runyonesque Harold Rosenberg, the luminous Hannah Arendt, and the local anti-Aristotlean David Grene. It also included two links to anthropology that meant a great deal to me: Victor Turner, who had left the Anthropology Department to spend most of his time in the Committee on Social Thought (to work out his newly discovered interests in 'liminality' and 'communitas' and to exorcise the ghost of Max Gluckman from his system), and James Redfield, the prodigy-classicist and son of Robert Redfield, who had begun to infuse his studies of Homer and Aristotle with an anthropological sensibility. This galaxy of loosely knit virtuosos presided over a skeletal programme of 'great books' and left it to the graduate students to find out how to get 'trained' in the ways that a normal PhD required. They were concerned with great minds (including their own), great books, and high thinking. Actual courses, useable knowledge, professional credentials and certification were our problem. They owned the charisma, it was ours to manage the routine. Many students in this strange programme disappeared without a trace. Others survived.

In my case, I survived and showed bad taste in finishing a PhD in six years. I was still fuelled by my Indian sense that courses deserved to be completed, exams were for ranking, degrees were for jobs, and that gainful employment was the main sign of a meaningful life. In this I was greatly helped by the availability of the immense resources of the University of Chicago in the study of South Asia. I was able to take courses with some of the finest scholars in South Asian anthropology, including McKim Marriott, Bernard (Barney) Cohn and Milton Singer, and the much younger Ralph Nicholas. Of these, Barney Cohn became my mentor, model and guru. My dissertation committee, appropriately eccentric, consisted of Victor Turner, who passed away in Virginia in the late 1980s, Bernard Cohn, and the late A.K. Ramanujan. All teachers by example and bodily hexis, they let my rawness cook in its own way but set high standards that I internalised quickly. They lightly blessed my thesis, which subsequently became my first book, *Worship and Conflict Under Colonial Rule*, which was published, somewhat revised, in 1981, five years after I received my PhD. The book, in retrospect, contains the strange mix of obsession with detail, big thoughts about history and anthropology, and an effort to combine areal and comparative issues that still characterises my interests. The fact that Edward Shils was prone to viciousness and Victor Turner was always funny and generous had more than a little to do with my going the way of anthropology, rather than sociology.

Thus the University of Chicago in the early 1970s immersed me deeply in the traditions and debates of area studies. Under the influence of Robert Redfield and Milton Singer, there arose a conversation that linked some of its finest social scientists to the study of India, and of the remainder of the developing world. As a consequence, many emerging nations were examined with fresh enthusiasm for how they challenged conventional social science research. In some cases, as with the Middle East, South Asia and the Far East, this interest in postcolonial modernity was grafted on to earlier philological and humanistic interests. In other cases, such as those of Africa, Latin America and Eastern Europe, the base for these interests was in anthropology, linguistics and history. In all these cases, the interest in world 'areas' certainly came out of the strategic background of American interests in World War II and many important figures at Chicago came out of this background. However, at Chicago, especially because of the interest of Robert Redfield in the comparative study of civilisations, and in the differences between peasant and urban civilisations, area studies found its centre of gravity in anthropology and history, rather than in philology (as at some other major American centres for area studies) or in the harder social sciences, as in yet other universities. This meant that cultural and civilisational transformation, and the relationship of cultural specificity to global patterns of change, were central features of the interest in the great non-Christian civilisations. This could be seen in the importance at Chicago of the journal called *Economic Development and Cultural Change*, which was a major host to debates about culture and development in the 1960s and 1970s, especially.

Thus, even though I was immersed in the arcane secrets of the Western canon because of my location in the Committee on Social Thought, India was never far from my daily life at the university in the early 1970s. And even as I contemplated the fine points of Allen Bloom's translation of Plato's *Republic*, or learned from Hannah Arendt that Machiavelli was also a playwright and not just a major political thinker, I was taking courses and learning the professional craft associated with serious research on South Asia. Here the extraordinary resources of the library system at the University of Chicago played a crucial role, and it was in the stacks of the Joseph Regenstein Library that I discovered the mixed sensation of Borgesian infinitude and Foucauldian panopticism that a great archive can induce in its inhabitants. I have never lost the sense of what such an archive can do and mean for teachers and students concerned with the detailed study of a world region. And my professors were all, whatever their other differences, master navigators of this bibliographic ocean. My own voyages in these waters began during this period.

Chicago in the early 1970s, for a South Asianist, was especially full of excitement. Marriott was fighting on at least two fronts: convincing David Schneider that he was not a positivist, and convincing others that he had developed a more 'Indian' sociology than Louis Dumont. Bernard Cohn was laying the grounds for work in historical anthropology that makes all the more high-minded moves of the 1980s and 1990s in this field less methodologically innovative than his own early works. Marriott and Ronald Inden produced their then famous essay on caste systems in the 1974 edition of the *Encyclopaedia Britannica*, a kind of papal edict on the new 'ethnosociology' that they hoped to inaugurate. Stanley Tambiah arrived in 1973 (overlapping briefly with Nur Yalman) before he too went on to Harvard. Tambiah joined Marshall Sahlins and others to create a post-Schneiderian anthropology, influenced by Lévi-Strauss, Saussure and J.L. Austin. As far as students working in the social and cultural fields of Indian studies were concerned, Marriott and Cohn drifted further apart, as Marriott pursued an Indic sociology with ever greater zeal, and Cohn continued to expand his broad sociological approach to anthropology and history. A few students worked with both Marriott and Cohn, but most felt they had to choose. Milton Singer was already (perhaps always) the elder statesman, holding the institution together, staying above the fray, assisted by his growing interests in Charles Pierce's semiosis.

Edward Shils, Lloyd and Susanne Rudolph, Lloyd Fallers and a few others carried on, in the early 1970s, the grand inquiries of modernisation theory, institutionally organised in the 1960s in the Committee for the Study of New Nations, which had been started by such luminaries as Shils, Clifford Geertz and Fallers, among others. It was a golden moment for the comparative and interdisciplinary study of large-scale social change, new nationalisms, and new cultural styles. Clifford Geertz's edited volume *Old Societies and New States* (1963) captures this background richly, and is still worthy of close reading. In many ways, it brought together the spirit of Max Weber and Franz Boas in a way that allowed me, much later, to look at globalisation as a complex and uneven cultural ecumene. And the classic work by the Rudolphs, *The Modernity of Tradition*, published in 1967, marked a major watershed

35

in the empirical study of modernisation. This work marked the limits of a certain way of thinking about change in developing countries and opened the door to new debates between the cultural and developmental strands in Indian studies.

Area studies, in the first half of the 1970s at the University of Chicago, were a kind of crossroads for dialogues of many kinds, between the humanities and the social sciences, between practical and cerebral approaches, between quantitative and qualitative styles of research. They were a major concern of some of the University's most brilliant faculty and thus they were never considered marginal or exotic. This sense of area studies as a window into central processes of world history and social transformation never deserted me in my subsequent career.

Chicago was also a place of deep doctrinal debate concerning how best to study the world both carefully and comparatively. There were lively differences between major professors about what constituted a properly 'cultural' approach. Others fought over how important the study of the Mughal world was to an understanding of a colonial sociology of knowledge for India. There was much debate about the importance of deep knowledge of multiple regional languages. The question of whether models generated through the empirical study of one place could usefully be transported elsewhere was another source of lively argumentation.

But through all this, some basic principles about advanced research and pedagogy were shared and I am sure they are still with me. One was that the library was more important than the classroom. The second was that no argument could survive without a deep relationship to some geographically and historically specific archive. The third was that no social science could be produced without some reference to local concepts and ideologies. And the fourth was that colleagues from South Asia were a vital part of our world: Romila Thapar, M.N. Srinivas, and Ranajit Guha were among the galaxy of South Asian scholars who came to Chicago and made sure that we were always aware of what the finest scholars in India thought of what we were doing. So the seeds of many inter-active biographies were laid for me at this time. Through Bernard Cohn's links to Ranajit Guha, I was prepared for my later meetings with the younger subalterns, all good friends and colleagues to-day. Likewise, the recently deceased M.N. Srinivas (who was a dear friend of Victor Turner's from an earlier Manchester connection), was kind enough to be the Indian guide for my fieldwork in Madras city in 1973–74, and through him I met his star pupil in Delhi, Veena Das, in 1978, and have been learning from her work ever since. Thus, in and through several Western settings, including Chicago, conversations were enabled between Bombay, Delhi, Calcutta and Madras, thus bridging styles, contexts, theories and scholarly lineages which might not have met so easily in India in the 1970s and 1980s.

Later, when I took my first teaching job at the University of Pennsylvania, where I taught from 1976 to 1992, in the departments of Anthropology and South Asia Regional Studies, I encountered other scholarly styles and personalities which opened new horizons for me. Sanjay Subrahmanyam, already the *enfant terrible* of the Delhi School of Economics, came to Penn for a year, based on his already rising reputation, as well as thanks to the links between Alan Heston (himself appointed jointly to the department of Economics and the South Asia Regional Studies department that had been built by Norman Brown) and the late Dharma

Kumar of the Delhi School of Economics, Sanjay's teacher there. These links, combined with the presence of David Ludden (first as a doctoral student and later as a member of the History faculty) and a visit by Burton Stein to Penn in 1976, kept me aware of the hot debates and changing positions in the study of the economic *longue durée* of South Asia. At the same time, Penn's powerful commitment to a European form of Indology laid the basis for a vigorous debate about Orientalism which produced the edited book *Orientalism and the Postcolonial Predicament*, edited by Carol Breckenridge and Peter van der Veer. This book, and the year-long seminar at the University of Pennsylvania which led to it, culminated a decade of tension about whether classical Indology and a new postcolonial critical stance were in fact compatible.

In my sixteen years at the University of Pennsylvania (where there had been a powerful tradition of Indology but virtually no serious anthropology of South Asia), I found myself having to teach the basics of South Asian anthropology, including the key works of the period after 1945: those by Louis Dumont, Brenda Beck, André Béteille, Nur Yalman, and many others. This was my real period of self-training in the anthropological canon of South Asia. And in teaching it, I learned what was inadequate about it, and these worries are to be found in some articles I wrote about 'hierarchy' in the late 1980s. But I also learned in this period of training-through-teaching that there was no way to produce a fresh approach to the anthropology of South Asia without a detailed grasp of the monographic literature of the last fifty years and the debates contained in this literature. At Penn, I also learned a fresh respect for potential dialogues between anthropology and Indology, in conversations with Ludo Rocher about dharma, with Wilhelm Halbfass about Indian ideologies of hierarchy and classical forms of scepticism, and with George Cardona about the profound and hermetic world of Sanskrit grammatical traditions. At the same time, the presence at the University of Pennsylvania of such colleagues as David Ludden and Alan Heston helped me to keep my eye on the materiality of social life. This last impulse, combined with conversations with friends (such as Nancy Farriss and Lee Cassanelli), in Penn's famous Ethnohistory Workshop who worked on other world regions, laid the grounds for the ideas that found final shape in my 1986 edited volume, *The Social Life of Things.*

At the University of Pennsylvania, I also learned a curious double lesson about area studies. I learned how they can either be reduced to philology or expanded through more dynamic forms of cultural analysis. And I began to see a way to move towards the latter possibility.

This is the background against which, in the mid 1980s, Carol Breckenridge and I began a journey in the study of contemporary cosmopolitan forms which produced our (more than) decade long work on the journal *Public Culture* and my own gradual engagement with the transnational and the global. In brief, we found that much of what we observed in India starting in the period of Rajiv Gandhi's leadership was not being studied by social scientists: media, tourism, consumption, advertising, sport. A great deal of what seemed to constitute the Indian present seemed to have no space in area studies. Frustrated by this deficit and intrigued by developments in cultural studies in Britain, the United States and elsewhere, we created the journal *Public Culture* in 1988 as a space where area studies and cultural studies could challenge and revitalise each other. It was an ambitious project, without good institutional support or an adequate conceptual map, but, twelve years after its creation, we believe that it has provided an important space for thinking the global in the register of cultural specificity and lived materiality. Here was yet another space where I developed the interactive biographies I shared with other South Asianists, both from South Asia and from the 'West', many of them young and new voices, many from the worlds of media and cultural activism. In the Public Culture Project we sought to explore the South Asian present and its cultural forms.

Of course, in thus engaging the present, and in insisting that this present has much to do with the circulatory dynamics of the contemporary world, we have sometimes been criticised for forgetting the importance of history and losing our grounding in expert regional scholarship. We continue to worry about these criticisms. But I am not unhappy about my own part in this effort to put area studies and comparative cultural studies in a different dialogue. Diaspora, both in the life-experiences of many of its theorists, as well as in many of the essays in the journal over the last decade, has now become a word of general currency. We sought to give it some specific gravity and to complicate the idea that public spheres were neatly bounded national property.

In my own work, starting in the late 1980s and culminating in the publication of *Modernity at Large* in 1996, I made the transition from thinking about the transnational to thinking about the global. This book was begun while I was still at the University of Pennsylvania and finished after I moved back to the University of Chicago in 1992. Thus, the book was produced where I began my first encounters with the study of modernity and modernisation. These latter are, of course, vexed words, and there are those who prefer what I call the Vatican strategy, which is to solve problems by producing lists of proscribed words (such as modernity), while retaining other words that protect unexamined the axioms of their own religions. That has not been my own path. I do not mind recognising that I am still struggling with the dilemmas of modernisation theory, of reconciling multiple histories of the present with one another, and of treating the study of global process and area histories as mutually enabling rather than disabling. Max Weber, among others, had some of these worries and his shoulders are broad enough for me.

These are interests I continue to pursue in a very different University of Chicago than the one I left in 1976, with a new conversation in progress about millennial moralities, vernacular cosmopolitanisms, and new geographies of capital. At the University of Chicago, in the 1990s, I have been able to continue my engagements with the questions of comparison and context, through the Globalisation Project. Within the broader aims of this project, we were fortunate to be early contributors to a national debate about the future of area studies stimulated by the Ford Foundation starting in about 1995. At the University of Chicago, from 1996 to 2000, we were able to host a conversation about new directions in area studies, under the rubric of 'Regional Worlds'. This project sought to explore the tensions between the study of the *longue durée* and the study of the global present, and helped to set new agendas for the study of cultural specificity in a world of high velocity commodity flows and new forms of human migration. As area studies has come to be more critical of its underlying nationalist and developmentalist architecture, I was privileged to be part of conversations with colleagues from around the world who could see that globalisation posed a new set of optical and epistemological challenges and opportunities for area studies in the coming decade.

It is not simply South Asians, inside or outside the West, who are shaping a collective conversation through their interactive biographies. It is also our imbrication in the lives and work of colleagues and friends whose commitment to the study of South Asia springs from other, even more admirable, sources. In my case, they have included teachers like Bernard Cohn, friends and colleagues like Sheldon Pollock and Peter van der Veer, and my life partner Carol Breckenridge. They exemplify, so to speak, the West in the East in the West.

A short story like this one inevitably leaves out many other stories which give it its context and its meaning. At least four such stories deserve brief mention here. The first involves the many students I have helped to train as scholars of South Asia. Many of them are already colleagues from whom I get some of my best inspiration and from whom I derive valuable support. They too cross the lines between East and West, and their lives form a part of the collective horizon I hope to share. The second involves friends and colleagues who have always remained anchored in India and have helped me in crucial ways with their ideas and their encouragement. The third is a story that is just beginning to unfold, which involves my collaboration with a group of activist-intellectuals in Bombay, many of a younger generation, who are changing my course more unpredictably than they may realise. The fourth involves my links with the unusual global network of scholars convened by the Center for Transcultural Studies in Chicago, which has stretched my possibilities and critically indulged my enthusiasms for almost two decades. These untold stories remind us that no story is more meaningful than those others, in its neighbourhood, which form the condition of its telling.

In the end, some parts of all interactive biographies are irreducibly personal. And here I must return to my early years in

Bombay, where my father was a journalist for Reuters who abandoned his job to fight with Netaji (Subhas Chandra Bose) against the British in World War II. He brought an unlikely world of Malaysian plantation workers, Japanese journalists and admirals, Bengali intellectuals and politicians, Urdu-speaking INA (Indian National Army) soldiers and members of Netaji's own family, into our home in Bombay in the late 1940s and 1950s. He also spent his last years worrying about world peace and the possibilities of a world government, an interesting vision for a man brought up in a poor village in the Tirunelveli district of South India in the first decade of the twentieth century and educated only up to high school before he migrated to Bombay in search of work in 1916. He seemed to know something about why the global was always near at hand, if only we knew where to look, when to move and how to return. I am still trying to find out what he knew. In translation, that effort has taken a highly professionalised form. What mediates that form with its originating impulse is the web of biographies I have touched on in this statement. They do not constitute a high sociology. But they are more than a matter of individual biography or accident.

Afterword

I dedicate this short note to two extraordinary scholar-activists who died prematurely and recently, and whose lives exemplify the fact that though South Asia is an area of study, it is first of all a place of embodied struggles and profound examples of ethical scholarship. Their names are D.R. Nagaraj (Bangalore, India) and Neelan Tiruchelvam (Colombo, Sri Lanka).

43

2

My Place in the Global Republic of Letters

Partha Chatterjee

My earliest consciousness of the outside world grew out of my involvement with my stamp collection. Some thoughtful adult had presented me at the age of five with an album and a few postage stamps. I spent long hours examining the few dozen stamps I possessed. I learnt very quickly that, for instance, stamps that said Magyar Hopta were from Hungary (and that Hopta was actually Posta) and that Helvetia was Switzerland. But it was difficult for someone in my position to acquire new stamps. My father received no more than two or three foreign letters a year and even those were from boring places like Britain whose stamps carried nothing but the same boring picture of the queen—not even the name of the country! I tried to persuade my father to strike up a correspondence with somebody in Monaco or San Marino where they made those beautiful triangular stamps. He did not oblige. My grandparents lived in Dhaka, which was in another country, and they wrote frequently, but only on Pakistani postcards printed in green—no stamps!

But by then I had become aware of another insignia of the outside world: my uncles and older cousins who visited us regularly in Calcutta carried Pakistani passports with their photographs on them. I knew passports were necessary when visiting foreign countries, and I had already decided that when I was older I would acquire one. But it must have been somewhat confusing to think of my uncles and cousins as foreigners.

Although I was reasonably knowledgeable about other countries and knew of places like Trinidad and Tobago and Transvaal (they played cricket in those places), I distinctly remember that, when one spoke of 'foreign', one meant the West—Britain, Europe or North America. I grew up in the first decade after Indian independence, but our school books still talked a great deal about the British monarchy and about diamond mining in South Africa, cocoa production on the Gold Coast, and dairy farming in New Zealand. We had an atlas in the house in which most of the world was still coloured red. I sometimes went to the riverside in Calcutta where there would be rows of ships flying the flags of many different countries. I often went to sleep thinking of sailing in one of those ships in which white men and women would lounge on deck chairs sipping tall drinks and reading French novels.

I did study English in school. But the world of European literature was opened out to me through Bengali translations of the nineteenth-century classics. My favourites were Alexandre Dumas and Jules Verne, and I loved to sit with my atlas plotting new routes for Philias Fogg's journey around the world. Apart from the books I was required to read at school, I read almost no adolescent literature in English. When I did begin to read world literature in English, I was already a precocious young adult spending long hours in the smoke-filled coffee house on College Street in Calcutta announcing my views on the novels of Franz Kafka and Albert Camus and the films of Federico Fellini and Ingmar Bergman.

In 1968, soon after my graduation from the University of Calcutta, I got a fellowship to do doctoral work at the University of Rochester in the United States. In Calcutta, the political climate was hotting up and the Maoist upsurge was round the corner. On university campuses all over the Western world, '68 had broken out. In the middle of all this, I studied political science in an ultraconservative department that took pride in introducing rational choice theory into political analysis. I didn't mind, because even though I was completely unpersuaded by what my professors taught me I enjoyed the mathematics. I spent much of my time exploring the stacks of the university library: that was an educative experience no Indian institution could have given me. Outside the library, there was the whole world in microcosm. I met, made friends and quarrelled with students from all over India and Pakistan, and from all over Asia, Africa and Latin America. In the heady days of anti-war student demonstrations, swaying to the music of Bob Dylan and Joan Baez, outraged by the murderous acts of the US government, ennobled by the heroism of the Vietnamese people, I discovered on an American campus the emotional experience of Third World solidarity.

However, I did not write my dissertation on India or the Third World. I wrote on the international states system, its emergence in seventeenth-century Europe, the balance of power, imperialism, the nuclear arms race—strategic game-theoretic models spiced with diplomatic history. Looking back, I do not remember having made any great emotional investment in my work: I must have regarded it as one more examination that one had to pass. Within weeks of defending my thesis, I was back in Calcutta, looking for a job. In February 1972, I got my first teaching job in India.

I don't think there was ever any question in my mind that India was where I should live and work. Perhaps the experience of graduate school in the United States taught me that, despite the unquestionably superior infrastructure and resources of academic institutions in the West, they could not nourish my intellectual and emotional life whose roots lay in the speech, activities, languages, hopes and fears of people I regarded as my own. It would be wrong for me to suggest that this identification was in any way a personal one, based on face-to-face knowledge, although, as I will soon describe, I did embark on intensive travel, both physical and textual, through the towns and villages of Bengal. The identification was anonymous, one might even say abstract, mediated by recognitions and desires that sprang from what I can only describe as an inherited cultural repertoire that, somewhere along the line, had received a certain political impulse.

I was fortunate to find a position in a new research institute that opened in Calcutta in 1973. My colleagues were mostly senior economists and historians, often with activist backgrounds in the communist party. They were hugely knowledgeable about libraries, archives, sources, texts, statistics and oral histories. I immersed

myself in the study of Indian history and society, Bengal in particular. I also teamed up with a colleague to study the rural locations
of the nationalist movement. That took me into every district of
West Bengal, by train, bus and on foot. It showed me my place
among the people I thought of as my own.

After my return from the United States in 1972, I did not leave
India for the next ten years. I kept up with the intellectual fashions
of the West. Marxism was in vogue at the time and exciting new
books appeared in the Calcutta bookshops every few weeks. We
discovered Gramsci, Althusser and Foucault. We waited for the
latest issues of the *New Left Review, Economy and Society* and the
Socialist Register. We also read Hegel and Marx, closely, studiously,
knowing even then that while the fashions would come and go,
these would remain the solid foundations of our intellectual dealings with the West. I studied agrarian history and the nationalist
movement. There was a new interest in the peasantry in the Western academy which rediscovered Kautsky, Lenin and, unexpect-
edly, the late Marx. All this was very exciting, but only because they
provided new ammunition in debates that were being conducted
in Indian politics. The Maoist uprisings had been beaten back and
along with it much of the Left. Indira Gandhi had uncovered the
most brutal and repressive face of the Indian state, but had also
managed to carry with her a part of the Left. Political writing had
become a serious and sometimes dangerous business. Now social
science research in India could only stay relevant by becoming
more, not less, political.

Subaltern Studies was born in this milieu. Some of its original participants were finishing their doctoral research in Britain
and Australia. A few now came back to work in India. Most of us

published in India, for an Indian readership. Some also published in Indian languages. In Calcutta I was already a recognised social science writer in Bengali. I still do not fully understand how my work, along with that of other members of *Subaltern Studies*, became known to scholars outside the field of South Asian studies. One of the proximate reasons, I know, was the emergence of Postcolonial Studies on American campuses in the 1980s, although this, as far as I am aware, was a trend largely confined to the literary disciplines. There was also at this time a new interest in several of the social sciences in the subject of nationalism, and here our work came to the attention of some scholars. By the late 1980s I was being invited to give talks and attend conferences in the United States, Britain and Europe. I also accepted invitations to teach for a semester at a time at the New School for Social Research, the University of Michigan and, most recently, Columbia University.

I do not feel these travels have relocated me in any way. I have grown more conscious than before of addressing different audiences. In India, this was always true in terms of writing in English as against Bengali (besides subtler differences such as writing for newspapers as against academic journals). But now I have become aware of specific disciplinary and cross-disciplinary readerships, the current state of the debate in those disciplines (although, despite my frequent contacts with Western campuses, I never quite manage to stay up to date) and a certain comparative and global perspective. I doubt that this has affected in any significant way the manner in which I look at and participate in Indian debates, except for the fact that I am now far more sceptical than I was before of claims to Indian uniqueness. If my views on Indian history and politics have changed over the years, they have done so in relation to changes in the Indian debates themselves, not because I have brought a different perspective to them. My place in the global republic of letters is, I realise, now marked forever by my nationality.

There was a time in my youth when this would have upset me greatly. When I wrote my doctoral dissertation at Rochester, I was especially concerned not to write as an Indian scholar. I was after all contributing to the theory of international politics and why should it matter what my nationality was? That was something I thought was best left to Indian diplomats at the United Nations (and in any case, I was not an admirer of the official Indian foreign policy). But over the years I have come to acquire and cherish a critical perspective on Western social theory that has emerged from my continuing attempts to study, understand and engage with the lives of the peoples of my country. I have learnt to relativise, to define the limits and identify the conditions of possibility of the universalist claims of that body of theory. Even when I write of Hegel or Marx, Locke or Rousseau, Gramsci or Foucault, it is hard for me to write except in relation to episodes and experiences that are, as it were, always at a tangent to, if not entirely beyond the margins of, what those great thinkers were writing about. It was in the course of engaging with the historically produced realities of Indian life, as much as negotiating my place in the global republic of letters, that I discovered that I had turned into an Indian scholar.

Curiously, my greater familiarity with Western academic institutions has made me less rather than more anxious about my inability to keep up with the latest. This is a worry that afflicts all academics in countries like India, and I myself suffered from it in my younger days. The modern social sciences in India have never been isolated from the Western academy in the last hundred years, but a feeling of backwardness, of lagging behind, has been pervasive. This was compounded in the decades after independence by the woefully thin distribution of infrastructural support that accompanied the huge expansion in higher education. Except for a tiny minority located in half a dozen favoured universities and institutes, social science teachers in India do not have even the minimum access to books, journals and data sources that would allow them to participate in the research activities of an international community of scholars. But the benchmarks, the references, the keywords, the corpus of texts that must be addressed, are always being produced out there in the metropolitan centres of learning, and by the time you manage to get your hands on one set of readings you realise that they are already out of date.

As I said, I used to worry a great deal about this inadequacy in my younger days and tried to work out with my colleagues various stratagems to keep up with the latest books and journals. Working from Calcutta, the problem is still with me, perhaps made worse by the mounting dollar prices of journals and our inadequate access to the electronic communications technology. But I don't worry about it any more. I know my work will always move on a tangent to what is being done at the metropolitan centres. It will speak to that constantly expanding body of research, learn from it, but never be of it. Being both in and out, and at the same time being neither quite in nor quite out, is a matter of constant negotiation. At the moment, as a putative citizen of the global republic of letters, I suspect I have less than one vote.

3

Off-centre: Feminism and South Asian Studies in the Diaspora

PURNIMA MANKEKAR

L ike many scholars of South Asian descent located in the 'West', my intellectual trajectory has been mediated by my experience of immigration and of living and teaching in the diaspora. Put simply, my life as an immigrant in the US has shaped my scholarly and pedagogical engagements with India and, more broadly, with South Asia. At a personal level, India is not simply a space on the map,[1] but has been the place of my childhood;

as such, it is the locus of memory, longing, desire, and anxiety; a real and an imaginary homeland (Rushdie 1991).[2] My relationship with India has been shaped by formulations of the politics of 'home' and location in US feminist scholarship during the 1980s, the time over which I was coming to age, as it were, as an academic.[3] Chandra Talpade Mohanty has argued for a reconceptualisation of 'home' as 'not a comfortable, stable, inherited and familiar space, but instead as an imaginative, politically-charged space where the familiarity and sense of affection and commitment lay in a shared collective analysis of social injustice, as well as a vision of radical transformation' (1993: 353). A politics of location entails the examination of how one's perspective and subjectivity are shaped by one's complex positioning at 'home'. Caren Kaplan points to the specifically North American provenance of the term politics of location (1994: 139) and, together with other feminist scholars like Mohanty (1993), Rich (1986), Hooks (1990), and Pratt (1984), points to its usefulness in carefully accounting and deconstructing claims to affiliation and identity[4]—whether those of gender, race, nationality, or sexuality. My engagement with South Asia is shaped by a politics of location stemming from multiple subject positions—including that of a South Asian immigrant living and teaching in California; a middle-class, urban-educated woman raised as an upper-caste Hindu; and as a feminist who feels strong ties of accountability to scholars and social activists in India. My positioning *vis-à-vis* South Asian studies as practised in the US has been shaped by my understanding that a politics of location, far from nostalgically seeking one's roots or being complacent about where 'one belongs', involves interrogating one's privileges and blind spots (Pratt 1984; Martin and Mohanty 1986).

It is no accident that I have chosen to base my primary field-work among communities in India and the Indian diaspora in the US. I stumbled into anthropology because of my interest in mass media, but I always knew I wanted to work among South Asian communities. When I first came to the United States in 1982, it was to study applied communication research. My objective, at the time, was to learn communication strategies for development projects in India. Within days of starting classes, I realised I was in a field that, for the most part, was oblivious to questions of culture and history, and was so unequivocally US-centric that area studies, or for that matter comparative studies, would have no place. On the rare occasion when it was addressed at all, culture was reduced to 'context' or to quantifiable 'dependent variables'. Conceived as a land of underdevelopment, 'tradition', and stasis, India was interchangeable with other parts of the so-called Third World. For a communications scholar, India could have been the ideal place to study and learn. Certainly, the India of my childhood had been saturated by a whole range of mass media: in addition to 'folk' and 'indigenous' performative traditions and public cultures, India was home to the largest film industry in the world; moreover, it had a thriving and diverse press, a nascent television industry, and large and heterogeneous literary traditions. The field in which I found myself, however, was a glaring example of the consequences of an absolute dismissal of area studies and critical cultural theories. Since I had come to the US with great expectations and enrolled myself in a graduate programme, I resolved to finish my course work as quickly as possible and, with the support of a sympathetic adviser, returned to India to do field research in a village in Haryana. My objective was to study a rural health care campaign launched by Unicef. I immersed myself in fieldwork, and wrote a thesis that was largely (and inadvertently) anthropological.

It was soon after I finished my master's thesis that I decided to pursue my interest in mass media in South Asia in the discipline of anthropology. With its emphasis on cross-cultural study and hist-orical context, and its tradition of fieldwork, anthropology seemed most conducive to my intellectual goals. It was in this context that I first encountered South Asian studies. Obviously, South Asian studies, as practised in the US, is now a lot more heterogeneous than what I was exposed to in graduate school. However, then, I was introduced to a South Asia I just could not recognise. Even granting that my experience of South Asia had been shaped by an urban, middle-class upbringing, this was not a South Asia that I believed existed any more—if, indeed, it had ever existed. This was an India where caste was the sole lens to study social inequality,[5] where women were either goddesses or hapless victims; where poli-tics could be understood either through the discourses of élites and leaders or through quantified election results; and where societal tensions were reduced to primordial conflicts ('from time imme-morial') between religious communities. In contrast, I was excited by the work of the Subaltern Studies collective, which had already left its mark upon debates on history and historiography in India. I remember bringing up feminist perspectives in class one day, and being told that it represented a 'Western' point of view and that my mission was to apply an 'indigenous' framework to my research— as if this 'indigenous' framework was singular, frozen in time, untouched by global events or currents of thought!

I know now that the kind of South Asian studies that I was then exposed to had been shaped by the historical contexts that engendered area studies in the US, and by assumptions about the ineffability of cultural difference.[6] Recent critiques situate the growth of area studies in the US in a specific historic and geopolitical context following World War II, when the US was attempting to consolidate its dominance (see Rafael 1994 for a careful elaboration of these contexts). Dipesh Chakrabarty describes area studies as an 'American reading of an older connection between liberal education and empire' (1998: 458). He adds that the epistemological bases of area studies were decidedly Eurocentric. 'What made these Eurocentric assumptions invisible', he adds, 'was in part the fact that area studies were still a matter of studying cultures that were considered "foreign" ' (1998: 459). Indeed, assumptions about cultural difference continue to be foundational to many models of area studies. As Rafael argues, 'Area studies conceive 'areas' as if they were natural—or at least, historically necessary—formations for the containment of differences within and between cultures' (1994: 91). Although about a decade ago I lacked the knowledge to understand why this was the case, is it any wonder that the India that I then encountered in my classes seemed so foreign to me?

At the same time, this was also when I was introduced to the potential of ethnography by one of my teachers, Val Daniel, an astute ethnographer and witty story-teller. His book, *Fluid Signs: Being a Person the Tamil Way* (1984), introduced me to the magic of ethnography, and remains one of the most powerful influences on my training as a South Asianist. My intellectual growth was fuelled by scholarship produced in both India and the United States—I found it exciting, productive, and necessary to keep my feet, so to speak, in both sites. It was then that I was introduced to some extremely exciting feminist historiography published in India. *Recasting Women: Essays in Colonial History* (1989), edited by Kumkum Sangari and Sudesh Vaid, made a powerful impression on me and provided the foundation for my own theorisation of colonial and nationalist discourses in India. In particular, Lata Mani's contribution, 'Contentious Traditions', reinforced to me the power of feminism as a mode of analysis. (So many years after its publication, this collection, and especially Mani's article, continues to be required reading in several of my South Asia classes and my courses on nationalism, colonialism, and postcoloniality.) This set of essays, as well as subsequent work by Rajeswari Sunder Rajan, Uma Chakravarti, Kumkum Sangari, and Susie Tharu, enabled me to forge my own feminist framework for doing South Asia anthropology. Furthermore, because of my interest in mass media and public culture, Arjun Appadurai's theorisation of transnational public spheres provided me with crucial conceptual tools for understanding the relationship between media and culture (1996). And the work of Akhil Gupta and James Ferguson (1997) opened up new paradigms for analysing the relationship between space, place, and culture—something I knew I would have to think through if I was to study mass media, with its translocal reach and its power to reconfigure the relationship between space, community, and identity.

As I struggled to formulate a project for my doctoral dissertation, I frequently drew on my own experiences growing up in India. For, despite the fact that I was living in the diaspora, my emotional, intellectual, and political ties with people, communities, and events in India were to powerfully shape my research. It was the 1980s and India was in ferment—more so, it felt to me, than in past years. Mass media in general, and television in particular, had become an overt instrument of 'nation building', but what the nation was to be, the content of national culture, had become the object of contentious debate and, at times, violent conflict. Even more agonising to me was how hegemonic nationalist ideology had shifted decisively, unmistakably, irrevocably to the right of the political spectrum: Hindu nationalism was becoming more mainstream. We were also witnessing an upsurge of Sikh nationalism: its (attempted) repression by the Indian state unleashed a decade of bloodshed in which thousands of innocent people lost their lives. The early 1980s were marked by two other important developments: the liberalisation of the Indian economy, and the introduction of entertainment serials on state-run television or Doordarshan (see, also, Rajagopal 2001). I knew, intuitively, that there were important connections to be traced between these apparently disparate developments. Every time I went home on visits, I was confronted with profound ideological and cultural transformations taking place in the public sphere but, to my knowledge, there had been relatively little effort to tie these developments together in the North American literature on South Asia. This was in dramatic contrast to the outpouring of cultural analyses conducted by intellectuals of various hues—historians, literary theorists, political scientists, economists, and activists—living and working in India.

I was particularly interested in the role of television in the (re)constitution of notions of Indian Womanhood. It took some work to convince my teachers and advisers of the anthropological significance of my project but, on my part, I had few doubts. For one, the links between this project and my own development as a woman who had grown up in India were inescapable. Like many other women of my age and class, my perspective on the world had been informed by newspapers and television; my sense of self had been shaped by novels, films, and popular music. But at the same time that I was an avid consumer of mass culture, I was always curious about its social and political consequences. And as someone especially concerned with women's experiences and lives, I was passionately interested in how mass culture shaped their aspirations, identities, and their ability to understand their world. I believed that women are not passive consumers of mass culture, and was curious about the different ways in which they actively engage mass media.

But most of all, I was concerned about the place of television in the growth of Hindu nationalism. I saw my research on Indian television as a feminist intervention in the 'culture wars' taking place in India over the subject and content of 'national culture'. In a very fundamental sense, this research, and the book that resulted from it, was targeted not only at scholars of South Asia, anthropology, and the cultural studies of mass media in the US, but, equally, at scholars, activists, colleagues, and friends in India (Mankekar 1999). As Mani has suggested in her reflections on presenting her research on nineteenth-century debates on sati to audiences in different parts of the world, such a project is neither easy, nor without traps and pitfalls but, instead, necessarily and inevitably involves 'multiple mediations' (1989).

Chakrabarty argues that 'critical scholarship requires us to imagine and locate a site where we can effectively intervene; hence one might argue that critical scholarship is committed to the *production* of a space within which it situates itself' (1998: 463, my emphasis). My book on Indian television was merely one part of a larger movement to re-envision South Asian studies—I have hardly been alone; there is now a burgeoning body of literature that seeks to recast South Asian studies in North America. Indeed, it is fair to say that, in recent years, South Asian studies have undergone quite a metamorphosis as a new generation of postcolonial scholars, trained in India as well as in the US, has begun to assert itself and make its voice heard in academic conferences, journals, classrooms, faculty meetings, and university-wide curriculum committees. This cohort of South Asianists, myself included, has been pushed to do so in no small measure by our students (many of whom are either from South Asia or are the children of South Asians who migrated after 1965) who would laugh us out of the classroom if we were to teach them only what we learnt in graduate school.

My students' gentle prodding, combined with my own fraught negotiations of my ties with India and my life in the US, has led me to engage issues pertaining to the South Asian diaspora. My current project examines how transnational public culture enables persons and communities in *both* India and the diaspora to '(re)imagine' India. Visweswaran notes that 'as "hybrid" or "hyphenated", "halfie" or postcolonial anthropologists begin to renegotiate the terms of distance and intimacy informing social analysis, theory itself begins to change, leading often to a strategic redeployment of experience' (1994: 235). My current project is shaped by my experiences as an Indian woman living in the diaspora and as a feminist activist working with issues of domestic violence in the South Asian community in the San Francisco Bay area.

In trying to build a life for myself as an Indian American immigrant in the US, in negotiating the daily pathways of my life as an Indian woman torn between two cultures, I soon realised that I was not alone in my efforts to juggle my ties with *both* my homes. I was struck by the immense power of public culture in mediating the lives of immigrant women in the US. Mass media seemed especially salient for women of Indian descent. Woman after woman I met spoke of how her ideas about ideal womanhood, her duties as a mother and wife, and her sense of what she could (or could not) do to change her situation was shaped by Hindi films, her engagement with Indian community events, the Indian songs that she listened to. I learnt that transnational public cultures, especially films, television programmes, newspapers, and public cultural events provided overseas Indians with crucial links with their homeland—whether it was their hometown, their state, or the India of their fantasies. Even when their relationships with India were ambivalent (as in the case of women who felt they had attained 'freedom' by emigrating) or antagonistic (as with those Sikh, Muslim, or Christian women who felt that the contemporary Indian nation-state threatened their personal and cultural existence), they could not shrug off these links. And yet, the India that women (and men) in the diaspora were imagining had itself undergone rapid transformations after the expansion of transnational mass media in the early 1990s. The lives of women in India and the Indian diaspora in the US are, of course, shaped by their specific cultural contexts, class positions, and sociopolitical locations. But do discursive practices of gender, tradition, and community travel between India and its diasporas? How are the lives of immigrant and second-generation Indian American women living in the US shaped by notions of 'Indian culture', authenticity, and woman-hood? Similarly, to what extent are the subjectivities of young women living in India shaped by transnational representations of gender and sexuality? In what ways do transnational public cultures enable this traffic in culture, images, information, and commodities? Since women form a crucial part of the 'audience', do their engagements with public culture enable (or hinder) their ability to build community in both sites?

This project is part of a larger movement within contemporary South Asian studies to refigure the field by attending carefully to questions of postcoloniality and globalisation (for instance, Appadurai 1996, Chakrabarty 1998, Gupta 1998). What does it mean to produce 'Indian culture' outside India—for example, in Southall, UK, or Sunnyvale, USA? How do these productions (and renegotiations) of Indian culture outside the geographical boundaries of South Asia compel us to revise our understanding of South Asian studies? Along with several other scholars, I am trying to formulate a vision of South Asia that brings area studies into conversation with analyses of transnationality, globalisation, and diaspora.

NOTES

1. I allude, of course, to Adrienne Rich's famous words: 'A place on the map is also a place in history within which as a woman, a Jew, a lesbian, a feminist I am created and trying to create' (1986: 212).
2. Obviously, Salman Rushdie's experiences have been shaped by his life as a South Asian living in Britain. By citing him here, I do not wish to imply a homogeneity of 'diasporic experience' or equate my experiences as a diasporic scholar with his, but simply to suggest that his notion of 'imaginary homelands' seems to resonate with my attempts, as well as

those of some of my informants, to invoke a purported homeland that we might craft through our imagination. Cf. Appadurai 1996 on the imagination as a social practice.
3. See, especially, Rich 1986, but also Hooks 1990.
4. As Caren Kaplan points out, the term 'politics of location' was 'a particularly North American feminist articulation of difference' (1994: 139). Kaplan rightly argues that, first articulated by Adrienne Rich in her interrogations of her subject position as a North American, white, feminist, the politics of location has since been appropriated in different ways, some of which she delineates thus: 'A politics of location is most useful, then, in a feminist context when it is used to deconstruct dominant hierarchy or hegemonic use of the term gender. A politics of location is not useful when it is construed to be the reflection of authentic, primordial identities that are to be reestablished and reaffirmed... A transnational feminist politics of location in the best sense of these terms refers us to the model of coalition or, to borrow a term from Edward Said, to affiliation' (1994: 139).
5. This, despite the fact, that scholars in India, such as André Béteille, were working on different aspects of social inequality, in particular the intersection of caste and class.
6. Of course, it is important we not be over-hasty in attributing canonical South Asianist scholarship solely to North American and European scholars, thereby valorising 'indigenous' scholarship on South Asia, some of which has participated in the formation of an orientalist and colonialist canon.

REFERENCES

Appadurai, Arjun. 1996. *Modernity at Large: Cultural Dimensions of Globalization*. Minneapolis, University of Minnesota Press.
Chakrabarty, Dipesh. 1998. 'Reconstructing Liberalism? Notes toward a Conversation between Area Studies and Diasporic Studies'. *Public Culture* 10(3): 457–81.

Daniel, E. Valentine. 1984. *Fluid Signs: Being a Person the Tamil Way*. Berkeley, University of California Press.

Gupta, Akhil. 1998. *Postcolonial Developments: Agriculture in the Making of Modern India*. Durham, Duke University Press.

Gupta, Akhil and James Ferguson, eds. 1997. *Culture Power Place: Explorations in Critical Anthropology*. Durham, Duke University Press.

Hooks, Bell. 1990. *Yearning: Race, Gender, and Cultural Politics*. Boston, South End Press.

Kaplan, Caren. 1994. 'The Politics of Location as Transnational Feminist Practice'. In Inderpal Grewal and Caren Kaplan, eds, *Scattered Hegemonies: Postmodernity and Transnational Feminist Practices*. Minneapolis, University of Minnesota Press: 137–52.

Mani, Lata. 1989. 'Multiple Mediations: Feminist Scholarship in the Age of Multinational Reception'. *Inscriptions* (5).

Mankekar, Purnima. 1999. *Screening Culture, Viewing Politics: An Ethnography of Television, Womanhood, and Nation in Postcolonial India*. Durham, Duke University Press.

Martin, Biddy, and Chandra Talpade Mohanty. 1986. 'Feminist Politics: What's Home Got to Do with It?'. In Teresa de Lauretis, ed., *Feminist Studies, Critical Studies*. Bloomington, Indiana University Press: 191–212.

Mohanty, Chandra Talpade. 1993. 'Defining Genealogies: Reflections on Being South Asian in North America'. In The Women of South Asian Descent Collective, eds, *Our Feet Walk the Sky: Women of the South Asian Diaspora*. San Francisco, Aunt Lute Press: 351–8.

Pratt, Minnie Bruce. 1984. 'Identity: Skin Blood Heart'. In Joan Elly Bulkin, Minnie Bruce Pratt, and Barbara Smith, eds, *Yours in Struggle: Three Feminist Perspectives on Anti-Semitism and Racism*. New York, Long Haul Press: 11–63.

Rafael, Vicente L. 1994. 'The Cultures of Area Studies in the United States'. *Social Text*: 91–111.

Rajagopal, Arvind. 2001. *Politics after Television: Hindu Nationalism and the Reshaping of the Public in India.* Cambridge, Cambridge University Press.

Rich, Adrienne. 1986. *Blood, Bread, and Poetry: Selected Prose, 1979–1985.* New York, W.W.Norton.

Rushdie, Salman. 1991. *Imaginary Homelands: Essays and Criticism, 1981–1991.* London, Granta Books.

Sangari, Kumkum and Sudesh Vaid, eds. 1989. *Recasting Women: Essays in Colonial History.* New Delhi, Kali for Women.

Visweswaran, Kamala. 1994. *Fictions of Feminist Ethnography.* Minneapolis, University of Minnesota Press.

4

Crossing Borders and Boundaries

VASUDHA DALMIA

I came to Germany as a twenty-two year old. Little in my upbringing and education had prepared me for life in Europe.
On the face of it, I was a typical example of Indian middle-
class upbringing. I had studied English in a well-known girls' college in Delhi, as so many others educated in convents, and been
brought up to believe in the infallibility of English literature. My
favourite teacher in school had been an English nun, downright
in her opinions, sweeping in her judgements, upright in her gait.
She had taught us to read the newspapers, discuss politics, become
familiar with Jane Austen.

Living in a middle German city made me realise that my English education was barely skin deep. My way of life was coined much more by the orthodox Marwari household, modified and softened in its ways by my educated Kayastha mother from Lucknow, ways to which I lived in deep resistance, but which nevertheless remained my point of reference.

East in East

I had spent the first ten years of my life at home. My younger brother and I had not been sent to primary school at the express wish of my father. He had been a leading industrialist between the two wars and was closely connected to the cultural politics of Hanumanprasad Poddar, the founder of the Gita Press in Gorakhpur, a formidable bastion of Hinduism from the 1930s onwards. Tauji, or Uncle—as he was called by my generation—preached in fact a modernised version of traditional Hinduism, printed Sanskrit and Bhasha texts in the original and with translations (in easily accessible editions), and brought out a monthly journal in Hindi, *Kalyan*, which was widely disseminated. We were surrounded with this literature, we read our way into a number of the beautifully printed volumes, but most of all we avidly read the annual number of the journal, a thick volume densely printed and packed with stories, articles and some illustrations. Here the two ways of life, the Indian and the Western, were presented as opposed to each other in all essential dimensions. In the issue devoted to women (*nari amka*) I remember well the black and white illustrations which looked like photographs. On one side of the page were pictures of the Hindu woman, modest in dress and demeanour, counselling and serving her husband in graceful submission. Lined up on the other side of the page were pictures of the club-frequenting, Westernised woman in sleeveless dress, smoking, dancing with her husband and, we somehow recognised, self-serving, faithless. The West corrupted.

Besides, as my father often asked, of what use was a school and college education which turned out essentially similar products? There were scores of jobless MAs and BAs. He wanted us to develop our own individuality. He told us countless stories, one tale melting into the other, of transgressive gods who populated Indra's heavens and of the *rakshashas*, banished to the worlds below, who fought for justice and their own space. We were to be educated at home, mainly on Sanskrit grammar and religious texts. We had a young Sanskrit tutor who memorised Panini with us. We could soon begin to take the Sanskrit exams administered by the Sanskrit University in Banaras. I had worked out in my mind that, by the time I was twelve, I could attain their highest degree: 'sastri'. An 'acharya' could follow. I remember the lonely triumph of composing my first *shloka*.

We were to demonstrate our learning at a huge gathering of pandits in Calcutta. I have a mercifully dim memory of stuttering into the microphone and sharp recollections of the arguments between my parents which followed fast upon it. My mother managed to extract us from our somewhat haphazard education. We were thrust into school, a newly opened convent in the heart of 1950s Delhi, and with that into a colonial educational environment which took bare note of the newly-won political independence of the country.

West in East

I had learnt a little English and I had some knowledge of arithmetic. But the other children regarded my brother and me with suspicion and were quick to point out that we were not allowed to speak Hindi on the school grounds, not even during the recess. In a thousand barely tangible ways, we learnt to despise Indianness. Hindu gods and the ritual life at home receded, to be entirely rejected later. We had moved from one kind of hostility to another. We worked with colonial texts, memorised poems about the English countryside which was dotted happily with daffodils and fairies. Our history books, printed in England, taught us about the vital onrush of Aryans into the subcontinent, the Dravidians who gave way; we became acquainted with vaguely sketched portraits of Mughal emperors and then, larger than life almost, with Clive, Dupleix, Hastings, Bentinck, Dalhousie (the roads in Delhi, at this date still named after them, were a reminder that these generals, adventurers, and administrators still peopled the imagination of bureaucrats and diplomats), and then with the independence movement, which apparently just happened.

The way had been evened for a BA in English Literature: Chaucer, Spenser, Bacon (' "What is truth", said jesting Pilate and would not wait for an answer'), Shakespeare, more Shakespeare, the Enlightenment: man as the measure of all things, Wordsworth (*The Prelude*, the French revolution: 'Bliss was it that dawn to be alive'), Keats, Browning, Dickens, T.S. Eliot. Entering this world was sheer headiness, an entirely legitimate way of becoming the individuals we had been told to become.

West in West

But I was thrown off course in Germany. Once I had learnt the language and been granted admission to the university, I began to delve into German literature. I read the works of the romantics, accosted Novalis and his strange tale, Heinrich von Ofterdingen, the mysterious blue flower which he sought. I read Goethe's *Wilhelm Meister, Elective Affinities;* I discovered Thomas Mann's *Magic Mountain,* Kafka's *Metamorphosis.* German literature relativised English and its lone dominance of world culture, at least as we had been taught it. It opened up new worlds, of melancholy, of yearning, of different layers of being. But it was vast and I was just beginning to dip into it. I turned to Indology, as yet in an unreflective way.

East in West

Yes, there was a discipline devoted entirely to India. My Sanskrit was rusty but later Indian literature interested me. The German Professor of Indology was forthright in his rejection. Did I have Latin? No, but as an eager twenty-three, I was willing to learn. It would not be possible even then, he said firmly. It would take years for me to understand the approach. Besides, as he told my partner at a later meeting, I was a lady. I should stay with English. The professor for English played tennis, he said.

East in the West was an entirely Western concern. I continued then with my study of English, William Blake, more Shakespeare, and for the subsidiary subjects turned to German literature and to Ethnology instead of Indology; no one objected to that.

Meanwhile I moved to a university town in South Germany. Indology could mean different things in different settings. Here as a young adult, I once again encountered Panini and discovered the German reverence for the Veda. The professor of Indology here was an internationally recognised authority in these fields. His immense enthusiasm spilled over into his students. He was generous with his time, barely noting the Indianness of my existence. Panini had known about the zero suffix in the fifth century before Christ. This discovery had revolutionised, if not founded, the discipline of linguistics in the West. And the Vedic gods represented moral values which the world had not known in quite this way until then. Here was unexpected revalidation of my early education. I would devote my life to the study of these texts.

I re-learnt Sanskrit the Western way and cautiously ventured into deeper waters, into what they called philology. Once again, a heady experience, for this science of philology prised open words so that they revealed their innermost kernel. The accretions of centuries fell off as so much dirt. Armed with a good grammar and a dictionary we could thus pore over texts, over one line of verse, over a single Vedic hymn, for weeks on end, till the inner self of words was laid bare. If we could then connect these selves with each other, then the world of unalloyed feeling and perception, when gods and men inhabited the same universe of meaning, could become accessible to us. And so we went on, with great zeal, semester after semester. The wonderful tales enlivened dry grammatical reflections. It took me five years to realise that this was knowledge rooted in itself. It had little connection to anything else, it barely needed India. The raw material had been supplied in the nineteenth century.

Somewhere in between, I myself had acquired an MA from my former German university and begun to teach Hindi, mainly as language courses which were considered an appendage to the main course of study. And even as that, I was to realise slowly, they revolved upon themselves, leading nowhere. Painfully, I learnt to teach Hindi the way I myself had been taught German and Sanskrit. Perhaps I could write a dissertation on the compound verb in Hindi, prising open the secret of its combinations?

A linguistics degree in Delhi University was a technical impossibility. But, for various reasons, I did return to Delhi. As I ran from pillar to post, seeking employment, I was told that with my knowledge of languages I belonged in the university. However, all I was equipped to do there was to teach German. So I was appointed to teach certificate classes in the evening. If I wanted to stay on in the university, I needed a PhD. Yes, but research what?

West in East

The 1960s and 1970s had seen a great flowering of urban theatre. Folk forms had begun to be used, sometimes with reckless abandon, to create new theatrical modes and to address new issues. Brecht's epic theatre offered many possibilities to absorb these forms creatively. Here was German presence on Indian soil. I read his plays, his theoretical essays and reflections, I read Walter Benjamin. It was from Brecht I learnt what historicisation meant. I learnt about the importance of Chinese theatre aesthetics, of the epic form, of oral traditions, of Russian formalism for his own theoretical edifice. He was 'A child of all nations', as the second volume of Pramoedya Ananta Toer's great *Buru Quartet* is entitled in English.

Brecht's theatre was political theatre. I talked to theatre people, I met Habib Tanvir, the great pioneer in the use of folk theatre
in North India. My friends in theatre taught me to understand
something of post-Emergency politics in India. There was still
buoyancy in the air, hope of change. I researched laboriously, analysed the translations of Brecht's plays into Hindi, what the direct-
ors of Brecht's plays in India thought and said. Together with my
partner, I puzzled out the creative misunderstandings of theatre
traditions which made possible new combinations, which changed
the very premises of the encounter. But in the meantime new questions also began to be thrown up. When did modern Hindi drama
begin? What was the function of this drama? When did the prosce-
nium arch come to frame Indian drama, creating thus new illusions
of reality, of psychological verisimilitude of character and new
visions of the historical past? When did East meet West? It was
in Banaras in the nineteenth century, within the plays of Bharatendu Harischandra, that Western drama, and Shakespeare came
to coalesce with the newly created plays in modern Hindi. I wrote
my dissertation on Brecht in Hindi. I acquired a PhD.

East and West

Personal circumstances took me back to teach Hindi in my old
department in Germany, to re-learn Hindi literature. I had trudged
through the length and breadth of it in my childhood and youth.
For, though my mother had sent us to a convent school, she herself
had gone to college and university in the high noon of nationalism
and had ever reminded us of the importance of Hindi literature.
She had pushed some of us, while still in school, to sit through all

the Hindi exams administered by the Panjab University in Patiala and the Hindi Sahitya Sammelan in Allahabad. I had come into the reluctant possession, which I now discovered to be a treasure, of their highest degree. For the next fourteen years I taught Hindi literature, but with a new consciousness of its historicity, of its embeddedness in the politics of colonialism and nationalism. It was a different kind of teaching now. It was connected to Sanskrit, it was connected to contemporary scholarship in India.

As far as research was concerned, for the next years I was to stay in the nineteenth century, trying to understand how tradition had reasserted itself in colonial North India. I focussed on the figure of Bharatendu Harischandra in order to work out what it meant to be a Hindu in colonial India. Dense and intricate were the many modes of interaction, the many bylanes and alleyways. There were many wishes and agendas that I carried into this research, but my friends and foes knocked my thoughts around till I could acknowledge that India and the East had in their turn used Western notions of nation and the state, of post-Enlightenment notions of history, to reinforce and reassert themselves and to build new edifices of power. And thus it was also that Hindi literature had been born, as the autobiography of the nation, as the new story of an old people.

Over the years my students and I faced and tried to answer innumerable questions about the why and how of Indological knowledge, of East as taught in the West. Nineteenth-century Indology was still a strong presence, exerting great authority, enjoying great prestige. We needed to investigate what it was that had moved the great scholars of the last century. We needed to understand that the questions posed in Germany, then and now, were different from those posed in India. Yet they were of concern to each other.

Meanwhile there had come about a new configuration of colleagues in my old department. Both positions in Sanskrit, that of the professor and assistant professor, had been newly occupied. I shall remain ever grateful to the new occupants for their insights, their modesty and their sharp critique. It was from them and in the environment they created that I learnt to understand in greater historical depth the relationship between religion and society, the ever-changing role of religious and social institutions, understanding for the first time that traditions I had been taught to regard as monolithic consisted in fact of a multiplicity of autonomous and semi-autonomous strands. This was my introduction to religious studies.

We continued to meet and clash on several issues and at times we fought relentlessly. On the one hand, I think we all agreed that knowledge was a continuum which refused to be compartmentalised. What was old, clearly reached into the present and what was new stretched similarly into the past. There was no real cut-off point between classical and modern, between East and West. On the other hand, as I saw it, it had to be acknowledged that there were no utopias and no encounters innocent of the notion of power. Then as now, there have always been keepers of knowledge, sometimes self-appointed, from whom it had to be wrested and this itself was a never-ending exercise.

Working within the frame provided by the Western academy, the question I have needed to ask again and again is: On what basis do I myself collect the data for teaching and research, what is the validity of the conclusions drawn from it? Can the knowledge produced here be extracted from this context and continue to be regarded as knowledge in completely different social and political contexts? I have come to believe that resolving these issues in fact is also a never-ending process. The knowledge produced in the Western academy, as elsewhere, can only be tested out in various contexts, to see how it measures up to lived reality.

In the meantime, I have moved so far West that India lies to the West of where I am. I now teach in a university in California. Indian reality has also moved West and with the second generation of affluent Indians, born and brought up in America, there has come into being the need to understand the past and present anew. My students? A sea of South Asian faces. Clearly, there are many Indias now, and we can only understand them together.

5

Representing Rural India

AKHIL GUPTA

I f someone were to ask me to name the question that I have to answer most frequently in my professional life, it would be, 'Why did you decide to leave engineering to become an anthropologist?'[1] As a high school student in Jaipur I had never dreamed of becoming a professional anthropologist in the West. I had chosen science and mathematics as my subjects; my school did not even teach sociology or anthropology. After following my parents as an immigrant to the United States, I pursued undergraduate and graduate degrees in engineering. Between the economic safety so important to new immigrants in the US and the professions deemed acceptable for ambitious students in India, my choice of study was a foregone conclusion, especially given the fact that the only other suitable career was considered to be medicine, and I had neither the aptitude nor the interest to study biology.[2]

In 1979–80, between the time I had completed my master's degree in Mechanical Engineering at MIT and the start of my doctoral studies in Engineering-Economic Systems at Stanford University, I stopped out of school and spent some time in 'Bharat Darshan'.[3] The goal of this trip was to visit different development projects run by a range of voluntary organisations in Andhra Pradesh, Karnataka, Tamil Nadu, Kerala, and Madhya Pradesh. Travelling with a friend for six months, mostly in overcrowded second-class compartments of passenger trains and on buses run by various state transportation departments, I learnt of an India that I had known chiefly through images and the casual contact that urban, middle-class Indians have with the rural poor. Growing up in small company towns in eastern India that were often in predominantly tribal areas had given me early glimpses of rural Indian life, but this was the first time as an adult that I spent a considerable period living and travelling through very different ecological, economic, linguistic, social, and cultural landscapes.

I wish I could say that this trip resulted in an epiphany that clarified the course of my career. In fact, nothing dramatic really happened. But it did provide me with some concrete examples and images as I pursued the study of 'development' in an academic environment. More importantly, perhaps, it gave me a perspective that has shaped the manner in which I approach research questions to this day. One of the things this trip did was to reinforce my predilection for interdisciplinary work, as I saw how difficult it was to separate issues 'on the ground' into the neat compartments of academic work. And so, after doing nearly all the same coursework as doctoral students in economics, I unofficially studied political theory, anthropology, literature, and philosophy, all the while pursuing my PhD programme in the Department of Engineering-Economic Systems. Among the economics graduate students with whom I was taking classes there was a strong interest in 'alternative' economics, particularly in Marxist economics and in Ricardian economics through the work of Sraffa. Donald Harris, who used to teach the alternative economics courses at Stanford, was a popular lecturer who impressed on us the 'big' questions that were not then in fashion in the other tradition of economics, particularly the intimate interrelation between economic growth and income distribution.

These were some of the influences from economics that lay in the background for my own study of agriculture in western Uttar Pradesh (subsequently published as *Postcolonial Developments*). Other sources of influence came from the mode of production debate (see Thorner 1982 for an overview), the emphasis on the relation between structure, agency and consciousness found in the works of Raymond Williams, E.P. Thompson, Pierre Bourdieu, Anthony Giddens, and James C. Scott. The questions I began to ask were much more shaped by these sources, the French structural Marxists, and the contributors to *The Journal of Peasant Studies* than by the mainstream of South Asian studies. My introductory foray into area studies was at best haphazard, since I did it on my own and with little guidance.

Donald Donham, an Africanist who taught anthropology at Stanford, first introduced me to some of the thinkers mentioned above, and particularly to the work of the French structural

Marxists such as Maurice Godelier, Claude Meillassoux, Georges Dupré, Pierre-Philippe Rey, and Emmanuel Terray. The other
major influences on my intellectual trajectory were the feminist
anthropologists Sylvia Yanagisako and Jane Collier.[4] From them,
I learnt the importance of 'the everyday'. They emphasised that
one needed to pay attention to how forms of inequality were re-
produced through the mundane practices of social life.[5] It is this
emphasis on the everyday, the taken-for-granted, the usual, and
the routine that feminist anthropologists had seized upon in their
own work, profoundly altering how everything was studied, from
ritual and kinship to political economy. But there was another,
perhaps less well articulated suggestion implicit in such an emphasis, one that flowered as the influence of Gramsci and Foucault was
more fully felt in American anthropology. And that was the notion that the 'normalcy' of the everyday, the unremarkable quality
of lived inequality, always had to be produced, that what was remarkable about it was precisely that it appeared 'just so' to all social
actors. I found this observation—namely that the 'normalcy' of
everyday life might be odd, complicated, and fragile, an analytical
problem in its own right rather than a point of departure for social
analysis—to be a highly productive and invigorating insight that
led to many new avenues in my own research, particularly in my
investigations concerning space and place.

At the time that I was working on my doctoral dissertation,
Arjun Appadurai very generously shared with me a series of as-of-
then mostly unpublished papers that he had been writing, based
on his work on agriculture in Maharashtra. These papers opened
up a new vista for me as they offered me a model of how to combine a real engagement with South Asian studies with some of the

theorists that I had been reading. After closely reading this body of work,[6] I embarked more confidently in the direction of bringing together in my own scholarly writing Marxist and Weberian influences, political economy and theorists of practice, and eventually poststructuralist thinkers as well.

My first job after finishing my doctoral dissertation was in the School of International Studies at the University of Washington in Seattle. I went from an environment at Stanford where there was no formal programme in South Asian studies to one with a strong tradition and a distinguished centre. I was hired, moreover, to teach in the South Asian Studies programme then headed by the historian Frank Conlon, and which had among its social scientists the anthropologist E. Valentine Daniel and the political scientist Paul Brass. The late 1980s were a particularly exciting time in South Asian Studies in the US, as subaltern history and postcolonial studies were just beginning to be assimilated into the mainstream of teaching and scholarship. Subaltern historians introduced exciting new questions about 'culture' into the dominant paradigms of South Asian history, which were anchored in economic and social history, and postcolonial theorists, working in the wake of poststructuralist theory and the critique of Orientalism, also offered creative alternatives to the binary of colonialism and nationalism. Having read the work of labour historians, theorists of practice, Marxist structuralists, and feminist anthropologists, I naturally found the new directions in South Asian studies to be appealing. In fact, my first two publications, written even before I had read any of the subaltern historians, was a 'subaltern' critique of Skocpol's theory of revolutions using the Telengana movement as my case study, and a subaltern reinterpretation of the film *Gandhi*.[7]

81

In the discipline of anthropology, too, the critique of representation unleashed new energies, prompting a fresh wave of research and reflection that paid attention to textuality and inscription. Couched largely in poststructuralist jargon, and borrowing heavily from literary theory, it echoed many of the themes of the emerging field of postcolonial studies. This was a confluence that proved highly fertile in that it opened up many new questions and approaches for me. It was in this context that I edited two volumes on space and place in anthropological theory and practice.[8] While the temporal dimensions of culture had come increasingly under scrutiny by a generation of historically minded anthropologists and culturally minded historians, its spatial dimensions were not nearly as well explored. This intrigued me, especially as poststructuralist theory introduced a host of new spatial metaphors to social analysis, themselves influenced by thinkers such as Michel de Certeau, Georges Lefevbre, and Michel Foucault. I was fortunate to find a collaborator, Jim Ferguson, who in his interests and approaches was like an intellectual twin, despite the differences in our background and training. Jim also brought to our joint work his knowledge of Africa, and Southern Africa in particular, that enabled an implicitly comparative dimension in which it was not assumed that the second, unstated, node was the West.[9]

It is through these prisms that I rethought much of my fieldwork material. The result is a study of rural India that on the surface resembles a classic 'village ethnography'. Nucleated village settlements in particular have proved to be an alluring object of anthropological analysis in that they seem to present the perfect example of a 'small scale' society. This is an image of the rural that has been reinforced by nationalist imaginings such as Gandhi's. If not entirely closed and corporate, the self-sufficient village community has proved to be a durable icon of rural India (see Brow 1999).

When I went to do fieldwork, I thought I had found precisely such a place. Alipur was quite small (approximately 700 people); it was multi-caste, with artisanal as well as agricultural castes; it had Brahmins, Harijans, and eleven other castes all living in one settlement, though in distinct areas; it had a small Muslim population as well as Hindus; it had a few large landowning Thakur families but mostly middle and poor peasants, as well as a substantial number of landless households; it had upper-caste families that possessed little land and lower-caste families that were substantial landowners; and it had green revolution agriculture but was not intensely mechanised by labour-displacing technology such as tractors.

It turned out that Alipur was anything but traditional, small-scale, self-sufficient, or uncosmopolitan. It was a thoroughly modern place permeated by national and global fields of influence, connected and dependent on markets, ideas, and technologies that circulated widely throughout the world, and inhabited by people acutely aware of their own position within national and global systems of inequality. This is what led me to reflect on the spatial assumptions embodied in the idea of 'the village community' and think about the difference between doing a study in one village and studying a village.[10] My goal was to show how an analysis done in one location could clarify the role played by different scales in the production of 'locality'. If 'the village' is in fact a place, how is such a place produced? Any answer that did not take into account market forces, administrative systems, the state machinery, the mass media, and national and global technologies of production and consumption would not be very satisfactory. And, yet, if one does take into account all of these phenomena, then not much is left of the 'traditional village community' found in anthropological and nationalist imaginings.

In thus doing a village ethnography that exploded the boundaries of 'the village', I have attempted to show why the literature on globalisation and nationalism matters to the study of poor, subaltern people. I am convinced that we need to demonstrate that events, institutions, and policies that operate on a national or global scale affect the *everyday* lives of poor people in the Third World rather than just assuming that they must. More importantly, *how* they impact the lives of poor and subaltern peoples—their experiences, actions, and motivations—cannot be decided in advance but must be discerned through empirical investigation. My interest has been in exploring the relation between forms of subjectivity, as epitomised by the 'development subject', and structural inequalities of class, caste, and gender.

It is hard for me to visualise doing research in India, particularly in rural India, without experiencing a gut-level urgency of addressing questions of poverty, illiteracy, and mortality. Even today, as much as three-fourths of India's population may still depend in some way on agriculture for its livelihood, and close to half the country lives in endemic and unimaginable poverty. What kinds of demands does such a situation make of the social scientist? It is as if one were doing fieldwork in the middle of a civil war or a famine: if one were to write an ethnography of such a context that appeared to ignore or downplay the significance of those momentous events, it would be strange indeed.[11]

One group of people whose actions are incredibly important for the lives of the poor and subaltern that is largely missing in anthropological descriptions of villages are state officials. In doing fieldwork, it dawned on me that the state loomed large in the consciousness and activities of villagers. Talking about how to 'get your business done' in a state office, dealing with state officials, spending time in administrative offices, banks, courts, and police stations were all significant aspects of villagers' lives. Given how significant 'the state' was to the everyday lives of rural folk, it was surprising how few state officials have populated South Asian ethnography. Where, I wondered, were the electricity officials, schoolteachers, health officials, agricultural extension workers, and development officials? In the depiction of village life, such people have been 'taken out' of the analysis because most anthropologists have not known what to do with 'the state', and how to integrate these officials in the descriptions of 'village communities'. My next project, therefore, set out to study such state officials, focusing on the symbolic construction of the state through the everyday practices of bureaucracies. I studied two major offices: the Block Office, responsible for co-ordinating development activities for a unit of approximately 100 villages; and the Integrated Child Development Services (ICDS) office, which was responsible for providing health care and supplementary nutrition to pregnant women and children, and basic education and immunisation services to young children. My goal in this project was to try and understand how 'the state' is constructed through practices and representations produced and engaged by village people and bureaucrats.

In the canonical literature, if villages have been perceived as being rich in culture, states have been seen as being relatively poor.

The cultural analysis of states proceeds from the standpoint that the problem is of determining how states react or respond to challenges differently because of differing institutional histories and due to the variety of cultural interchanges with their respective civil societies. In other words, legitimation problems of states are often attributed to the fact that their economic systems may be out of synch with the political or cultural demands being placed on them. This was one of the big problems for modernisation theorists, who worried that new information technologies and popular democratic mobilisation would place strains on developing countries because the demands of these systems would outpace the ability of the economic system to meet those demands. 'The revolution of rising expectations', it was feared, would place demands on nation-states in developing countries that those states would be unable to meet, leading to widespread disaffection and political instability.[12]

In all these approaches, 'culture' is seen as external to states, as a source of problems or arenas of difference. I have approached this project from a completely different perspective. The starting point for my own analysis is the observation that states, as translocal institutions with multiple agencies, organisations, levels, agendas, and centres, and like multinational corporations or nations, have to be imagined. My research focuses on the means by which this process of imagining is realised for concrete actors at the lowest levels of state bureaucracies. My argument is that any process of imagining 'the state' involves the circulation of representations—speeches by politicians and bureaucrats, newspaper reports, but also files, orders, memos, applications—as well as the habitual re-enactment of representational practices of command and deference, inspection trips by senior officials, meetings, and the writing of reports. It is through such representations and everyday practices that states come to be imagined by bureaucrats no less than by the public. And these everyday processes of representation and action are saturated with struggles for hegemony. In other words, questions of legitimacy are intimately involved in the *constitution* of states, and not just a question that hangs over states in moments of crisis. Understanding the culture of states, therefore, is essential to any theory of the state, one moreover that lodges conflict, struggle, and inequality at the heart of how states are imagined and inhabited rather than simply in terms of the consequences of state policies and actions.

Notes

1. This is also one of the questions I have to answer most frequently among relatives and friends, some of whom to this day insist on introducing me as an 'economist', a characterisation that might make Alfred Marshall turn in his grave.

2. A number of other South Asian social scientists of my generation have also entered their fields after a primary post-secondary degree in the sciences or engineering. In my own case, training in systems theory and economics has helped in thinking about linkages between different scales and levels, made me appreciate the importance of combining different methods (quantitative and qualitative) in social inquiry, but also made me sceptical of the earnest efforts by some social scientists to find some statistical or mathematical technique to 'ground' the claims of social scientific research.

3. The term literally means 'a pilgrimage of India'.

4. Some of their work can be found in their jointly edited volume. See Collier and Yanagisako (1987). For other work, see Yanagisako (1985) and Yanagisako and Delaney (1995); Collier (1973; 1988; 1997).

5. I am not suggesting that they were the first to do so, merely that this emphasis was critical in my own intellectual history.

6. Unfortunately, although they well deserved to be, these papers were never collected into a book. See Appadurai (1984a; 1984b; 1989a; 1989b; 1991); related articles appeared in Appadurai (1986; 1988).

7. The critique of Skocpol appeared in Gupta (1984); the article on Gandhi is to be found in Gupta (1983).

8. The two collections have been co-edited with James Ferguson (Gupta and Ferguson 1997a; 1997b).

9. I would be remiss in not mentioning here Jim's great generosity, of intellect and spirit, that has allowed for the smoothest collaborative relation imaginable.

10. I borrow this line from Geertz, who described what anthropologists do thus: 'Anthropologists don't study villages (tribes, towns, neighborhoods . . .); they study *in* villages' (1973: 22).

11. It could be quite convincingly argued that the number of deaths that occur regularly in rural South Asia due to malnutrition and morbidity far exceed the casualties that might accrue through wars and catastrophic natural disasters. Hence, this case has closer parallels to the example of civil war and famine than may be apparent at first. The research of Amartya Sen and Jean Dreze has been especially helpful in focusing attention to these questions. See Sen (1983); Dreze and Sen (1995); Dreze and Sen, eds (1996).

12. The phrase 'revolution of rising expectations' is attributed to Galbraith. Among the prominent modernisation theorists who advanced such positions were W.W. Rostow (1960) and Samuel Huntington (1968). In Latin America, such positions were found in the work of Torcuato di Tella (1965) and Gino Germani (1978).

REFERENCES

Appadurai, Arjun. 1984a. 'Wells in Western India: Irrigation and Co-operation in an Agricultural Society'. *Expedition*, 26(3): 3–14.

————. 1984b. 'How Moral is South Asia's Economy?—A Review Essay'. *Journal of Asian Studies*, 43(3): 481–97.

————. 1986. 'Is Homo Hierarchicus?—A Review Essay'. *American Ethnologist*, 13(4): 745–61.

————. 1988. 'Putting Hierarchy in Its Place'. *Cultural Anthropology*, 3(1): 36–49.

————. 1989a. 'Transformations in the Culture of Agriculture'. In Carla Borden, ed.. *Contemporary Indian Tradition*. Washington, DC, Smithsonian Institution Press: 173–86.

————. 1989b. 'Small-Scale Techniques and Large-Scale Objectives'. In Pranab Bardhan, ed. *Conversations Between Economists and Anthropologists*. New Delhi, Oxford University Press: 250–82.

————. 1991. 'Dietary Improvisation in an Agricultural Economy'. *Diet and Domestic Life in Society*. Eds Anne Sharman *et al.* Philadelphia: Temple Univ. Press, pp. 207–32.

Brow, James. 1999. 'Utopia's New-found Space: Images of the Village Community in the Early Writings of Ananda Coomaraswamy'. *Modern Asian Studies*, 33(1): 67–87.

Collier, Jane Fishburne. 1973. *Law and Social Change in Zinacantan*. Stanford, Stanford University Press.

————. 1988. *Marriage and Inequality in Classless Societies*. Stanford, Stanford University Press.

————. 1997. *From Duty to Desire: Remaking Families in a Spanish Village*. Princeton, Princeton University Press.

Collier, Jane Fishburne and Sylvia J. Yanagisako, eds. 1987. *Gender and Kinship: Essays Toward a Unified Analysis*. Stanford, Stanford University Press.

Di Tella, Torcuato. 1965. 'Populism and Reform in Latin America'. In Claudio Veliz, ed. *Obstacles to Change in Latin America*. London, Oxford University Press: 47–74.

Dreze, Jean and Amartya Sen. 1995. *India: Economic Development and Social Opportunity*. Delhi, Oxford University Press.

————. 1996. *Indian Development: Selected Regional Perspectives.* Delhi, Oxford University Press.

Geertz, Clifford. 1973. 'Thick Description: Toward an Interpretive Theory of Culture'. In *The Interpretation of Cultures.* New York, Basic Books: 3–30.

Germani, Gino. 1978. *Authoritarianism, Fascism, and National Populism.* New Brunswick, NJ, Transaction Books.

Gupta, Akhil. 1983. 'Attenborough's Truth: The Politics of Gandhi'. *The Threepenny Review*, 15: 22–3.

————. 1984. 'Revolution in Telengana, 1946–1951'. *South Asia Bulletin*, vol. 4. Part 1: No. 1, pp. 1–26; Part 2: No. 2, pp. 22–32 (Reprinted in *Social Science Probings*, 3(1): 3–71).

————. 1998. *Postcolonial Developments: Agriculture in the Making of Modern India.* Durham, Duke Univ. Press.

Gupta, Akhil and James Ferguson. 1997a. *Culture, Power, Place: Explorations in Critical Anthropology.* Durham, Duke University Press.

————. 1997b. *Anthropological Locations: Methods and Grounds of a Field Science.* Berkeley, University of California Press.

Huntington, Samuel P. 1968. *Political Order in Changing Societies.* New Haven, Yale University Press.

Rostow, Walt Whitman. 1960. *The Stages of Economic Growth, A Non-Communist Manifesto.* Cambridge, Cambridge University Press.

Sen, Amartya. 1983. *Poverty and Famines: An Essay on Entitlement and Deprivation.* New York, Oxford University Press.

Thorner, Alice. 1982. 'Semi-Feudalism or Capitalism? Contemporary Debate on Classes and Modes of Production in India'. *Economic and Political Weekly*, vol. 17, no. 49, Dec. 4, pp. 1961–8; no. 50, Dec. 11, pp. 1993–1999; no. 51, Dec. 18, pp. 2061–6.

Yanagisako, Sylvia. 1985. *Transforming the Past: Tradition and Kinship among Japanese Americans.* Stanford, Stanford University Press.

———— and Carol Delaney, eds. 1995. *Naturalizing Power: Essays in Feminist Cultural Analysis.* New York, Routledge.

6

De-ghettoising the Histories of the Non-West

Shahid Amin

In July 1960, much before globalisation and the onset of academics jet-setting from the East to the West, my father, a medievalist teaching in a college in Delhi, took a ship from Bombay on a long journey to study South East Asian history at Stanford University. This was the second time in ten years that he was sailing to the US for a higher degree; independent India was then not quite in its teens, and American foundations were attracting the younger minds of the 'new nations' of Asia to study each others' and their own pasts in major centres of learning in the States. Unlike in England, where scholarships were scarce, mentors patronising, and concerns imperial-insular, Cornell and Stanford appeared far more inviting.

So, while father went West, the rest of the family—I was barely ten—took the train from Delhi, changing lines and gauges at the provincial capital of Lucknow, to settle temporarily at our ancestral home 520 miles east in the province of Uttar Pradesh. Deoria, tucked away in the north-eastern corner of the province, was the inconsequential headquarters of a new district: as children, we were told that both electricity and the district collector—the latter a visible sign of our small town having attained administrative puberty—came to Deoria in the same year. Strange and predictable are the ways of memory: our new district was officially sawed off from Gorakhpur in 1946, but it took some time to take shape. The town definitely received its power supply in 1949, and it is the difference made to quotidian and civic life by the 60-watt GEC bulb that cast its shadow on the remembered inexactness of the Deoria-born midnight's children.

Even in the late 1950s, a minion of the municipality would routinely clamber up a portable ladder—the sort that paid electoral publicists in India carry on bicycles for high-density poster warfare—to replenish and light the glass-encased oil lamps stuck on bamboo poles at the head of the smaller lanes. We associated these street-lamps with the word 'public': such was our adolescent municipal consciousness in an inadequately lit Deoria of the 1950s.

The other sign of the early maturity of Deoria town was the well-swept, red brick-and-tiled K.E. Higher Secondary School; the initials originally stood for King Edward VII, but the abbreviation, when rendered in the local language, was meaningless unless one chose to indigenise it as the Hindi word 'Kaee', meaning 'not one' but 'several'. The singularity of that imperial school, one each for every dusty district, was lost on us first-generation post-colonials, for we subordinated an historic nomenclature to the freedoms of juvenile wordplay.

Historic for its time and place, 'Kaee', Deoria, came as a culture shock to me, catapulted from New Delhi fairly early to negotiate my roots—in the place of my birth, no doubt, but miles away from the nuclear home. So it was as an adolescent in the early 1960s in faraway Deoria that I picked up the rudiments of north Indian languages, history and culture, and developed an affinity with a large patch of 'village India' that has remained with me ever since.

The mid-1960s, spent in a New Delhi school, were uneventful; it was 1968 and more specifically the Indian variant of Maoism associated with the peasant uprising in Naxalbari in North Bengal in 1967 that was the more important influence that helped shape my intellectual concerns. As with several colleagues who came together in the late 1970s to form the Subaltern Studies collective, even after the political challenge of the Naxalbari movement had been crushed the fundamental question of political power in post-colonial India that it managed to raise had important bearing on our understanding of India's colonial history. It led to a questioning of the quiet confidence, indeed the supreme and not quite warranted confidence, that the dominant ideology of Indian nationalism had hitherto exuded over a colonial past.

In the 1960s and 1970s economic history was the reigning sub-discipline within history. In the third world this was the period of debate around Andre Gunder Frank's conceptualisation of capitalist relations of production in the colonies in terms of relations of capitalist exchange. In India the main focus was on the specifically colonial causes for the failure of India to industrialise, and in understanding what came to be called 'semi-feudalism': this colonial hybrid referred to the tardy development of capitalist relations in agriculture, and an inadequately disruptive differentiation within the peasantry even after nearly a century of commodity production for the global and the national market.

It was this conceptual primacy of the national-colonial that Maoist political excess aimed against the post-colonial nation-state highlighted so dramatically. Paradoxical as it may seem, it was the voluntarism of the Indian Maoists that influenced a group of historians in the late 1970s to develop and apply the idea of the 'subaltern', borrowed from Gramsci, in historical practice. The intellectual impetuosity of the Indian Maoists stemmed from the perceived power of revolutionary theory. It was considered sufficient in those days to have digested Mao's celebrated *Report on the Peasant Movement in Hunan* or 'How to Analyse Classes in Rural China'; one did not need a nuanced understanding of peasants in India. The failure of the Maoist idea in practice by the 1970s made a section of the radical intelligentsia pay a good deal more attention to the peasantry in India in its political, social, economic and religious aspects, and question the historical claim of the nation to speak for its peasants.

As someone training to be a historian, I was already committed in the early 1970s to studying Chinese and Indian peasant movements; thanks to Ford Foundation funding, one could do a fair amount of Chinese history and language in Delhi itself. And so when I landed a scholarship at Oxford University in 1973 I had plans of comparing the agrarian society and politics of eastern

Uttar Pradesh and Yenan, no less! One of the first books that I bought at the famous Blackwells bookshop at Oxford was a copy of Matthew's Chinese–English dictionary. However, the rigours of advanced Chinese at the Oriental Institute at Oxford were enough to dampen my youthful political commitment to the history of Chinese peasants. So it came to pass that, thirteen years after my first involuntary encounter with the peasants of my ancestral home, I made a conscious decision to study my bit of the world as a historian and an anthropologist, marching outwards from the archives to engage in a dialogue with persons whose pasts and histories were very different from mine, but with whom I had a certain affinity nevertheless.

Balliol College, Oxford, was of course different from St Stephen's College, Delhi, where my father taught, and which nurtured many a young historian of India in the 1970s and 1980s. But the transition was made easier in my case, for in a manner of speaking, I had taken my mentor from India along: Professor Tapan Raychaudhuri, who initiated me into economic history at Delhi, had moved to Oxford in early 1973; I was to follow him a few months later. My nine long years in Oxford were certainly intellectually eventful, but I don't think I learnt my way of doing history at that old university. The great advantage of a long stay at Oxford was the ease with which one could ransack the colonial archive, in the wide sense of that term. The Indian Institute had open access to all the printed material on India; the India Office Library, that mammoth off-shore repository of our colonial past, was not far away. It was the fact that I was, as it were, at home with the colonial archive and kept returning to it after my frequent trips to the field, that afforded me, I feel, both a critical distance from the 'authoritative sources' and the freedom to experiment with my search for local records in India; and now that I think about it, it also made possible a dialogue with the present inheritors of past events in the locale of my historical work.

Funnily enough, my initial nine years in the West enabled me to know and write about my patch of the world in ways which might have been unavailable to me had I been entirely home-grown. This was aided by the fact that my long stay in Oxford gave me the opportunity of working closely with Ranajit Guha, who was at the University of Sussex, and from whom I have learnt most as a historian. So, apart from enabling me to research 'East' more intensively and unconventionally, my academic training in the 'West' owed a lot to a dialogue with 'Eastern' gurus of an earlier generation then resident in England.

Over the years my interest has ranged through economic history, linguistics, semiotics, law, anthropology and what I call 'historical fieldwork', i.e. the historian's endeavour to trace, analyse and narrate the diverse relations between records of the time and recollections of time past. My current research seeks to explore the tensions between historians' history and religious communities' sense of their own past.

My doctoral dissertation sought to provide an answer to the endurance of peasant family farms as the unit for the social reproduction of labour in colonial India. Since then I have written on colonial classificatory systems and the cataloguing of agricultural India; peasant constructions of Gandhi as a mahatma; rumours and their transmission in peasant societies; the ways of judicial discourse and its relationship to the problematic construction of first-person accounts in confessional statements of peasant rebels; war-time censorship and the creation of archives of fragments; the constituents of nationalist narratives; the refashioning of pasts in the histories of post-colonial nations, and the tension between official memorialisation and local and familial memories that this necessarily entails. My recent book, *Event, Metaphor, Memory: Chauri Chaura, 1922–1992* (Berkeley/Delhi, 1995)—the story of a violent peasant–police encounter in the career and mnemonics of non-violent Gandhian nationalism—combines archival research with 'historical fieldwork', a dialogue between the historian and the inheritors of historic events at the present site of past actions. It is located at the intersection of authoritative accounts, judicial and nationalist, and remembrances occasioned by conversations with a 'local historian'—the sort who travels halfway round the globe to talk to peasants of the neighbouring district—in a context changed not just by the passage of time but by the belated permission granted by the nation-state to narrate a particular 'crime' as politics.

My debts—intellectual, personal and institutional—to the West are of course many; my research into the continuing history of this day-long event was conducted largely in the villages and local record rooms of eastern Uttar Pradesh, but written over three years in active dialogue with historians and anthropologists in Europe and America. The commonality between my little history of the long afterlife of an obscure murderous event in the self-fashioning of a non-violent nationalist polity, and the event-based histories of the lives of ordinary people in early Modern Europe, is

97

obvious. However, it might be useful to sketch some of the differences.

With so much talk about the revival of narrative in the West, the concerns among some of us writers in India are not identical. It is not a narrow parochialism but a desire to critique the nation, make it habitable and write beyond it that, I feel, accounts for much of the difference. The pasts evoked in some of the classic event-based histories of early Modern Europe do not impinge on a contested national present in quite the same way as happens with a lot of critical historical writing from India. I have therefore found it useful to turn on its head Collingwood's idea of 'events which have finished happening'. Such windows of opportunity are more open where the distance between 'event time' and 'discourse time' is not fixed, but is contingent on the perspectives of alternative historical experiences, enterprise and projects. It is precisely this difference from the West that allows the possibility of such histories of the non-West to be radical alternatives to the very best that the master practitioners of (Western) history have to offer.

As elsewhere, so also in India, schoolbooks, political animals and jubilee celebrations all seek to construct the sense of an uncluttered national past. Revulsion at the idea of a national-plural is almost visceral with the majoritarian-nationalist, for it disorders a national past which they simultaneously consider historical and singular. Swimming against the tide enables the historian to ask an important question that we as a nation face about our pasts: is there something inherent in the ways of nation-states that makes it difficult for citizens to relate to history outside a mainstream and accredited version of the past—the national past? Can we at all remember without commemorating? Can we recollect without celebrating, recall without avenging? Why are national histories invariably encrusted in the lapidary mode?

Throwing a challenge to the nation-state's confidence over the framing of a common past, histories of what I call recalcitrant events—events which clutter the order of history—would have no prior claim on an already familiarised national readership. So, to read these histories within the nation would have the effect of defamiliarising that which is familiar national history. In order to be read, such histories would have to elicit permission to narrate what is already clearly seen as Not-History. In these 'new narratives', the 'how' of the craft of the historian is necessarily tied up with the 'what' of the story being told. Beyond the nation, these newer ways of historical narration may simultaneously help in making the unfamiliar (and a great deal of 'non-Western history' will remain unfamiliar in the West) accessible in non-stereotypical ways, i.e. in terms other than the time-tested categories and tropes of accounting for the pasts of the 'non-West'.

It is these newer forms of storytelling that might enable us to de-ghettoise 'histories of the East'. It is only then that we may succeed in writing not just recognisably Indian or South Asian histories, but events and processes that have India or South Asia as their location. To accede to the demand of making the unfamiliar accessible in familiar ways is to be complicit in the production of ghettoised mainstream histories.

Of course this is not an invitation to shift to historical fiction, but to write the 'historic'-unfamiliar in ways which elicits readers' assent both in the East and the West, even as it invites the charge of being Not-History from the guardians of Clio's estate.

REFERENCES

Guha, Ranajit. 1963. *A Rule of Property for Bengal: An Essay on the Idea of Permanent Settlement in Bengal.* Paris, Mouton.

———. 1983. *Elementary Aspects of Peasant Insurgency in Colonial India.* Delhi, Oxford University Press.

———. 1997. *Dominance Without Hegemony: History and Power in Colonial India.* Cambridge, Mass., Harvard University Press.

———. 1982–9. *Subaltern Studies: Writings on South Asian History and Society* (vols 1–6). Delhi, Oxford University Press.

Raychaudhuri, Tapan. 1966. *Bengal Under Akbar and Jahangir: An Introductory Study in Social History.* Delhi, Munshiram Manoharlal, 2nd edition.

———. 1962. *Jan Company in Coromandel: A Study in the Interrelations of European Commerce and Traditional Economies.* S'gravanhage, Martinus Nijhoff.

———. 1988. *Europe Reconsidered: Perceptions of the West in Nineteenth-century Bengal.* Delhi, Oxford University Press.

———. 1999 *Perceptions, Emotions, Sensibilities.* Delhi, Oxford University Press.

Raychaudhuri, Tapan. Co-edited. 1982. *The Cambridge Economic History of India*, 2 vols. Cambridge, Cambridge University Press.

7

Journey to the East, by the West

PRASENJIT DUARA

The Journey to the West is a much loved Chinese vernacular novel of the sixteenth century. It is based very loosely on the journey to India by the seventh-century Buddhist pilgrim, Xuan Zang, in quest of the Buddhist scriptures, truth and salvation. The novel features the monk Tripitaka, but its most popular character is his principal disciple and protector, the monkey, Sun Wukong. Although he is dedicated to the sacred mission and overcomes ogres, demons, and other appalling obstacles, Sun Wukong remains mischievous, wildly irreverent and filled with hubris. The story frames my essay not only because I reverse the

101

pilgrimage, but it is so full of ironies and reversals itself that many who read it may recognise their own lives in that journey.

Reflecting on an intellectual journey in our own time makes sense only as a history of the present. Surely like many others I face our historical present undecided and wavering: are we at an impasse or a crossroads? The critical historian in me is hobbled by the collapse of all salvation narratives accompanying the fall of actual socialism even as global stratification intensifies. The productive historian in me still hopes to identify the source of our problems—whether it be the state penetration of our lives, commodification of relationships, intolerant nationalisms—and work vigorously to imagine a world before, without, or around it; in other words, to embrace the possibilities in the new.

The history of my present begins most clearly with the appearance of the radical student movement in India of the 1960s and 1970s. As a student in Delhi I was fired by the utopian possibilities of the Cultural Revolution, which, in 1970, was still aglow in the rhetoric of that Maoist triumph: the 1969 Congress of the Chinese Communist Party. My classmate, Shahid Amin, has written elegantly in this very collection about the conditions and shaping influence of that movement upon our generation. We were the second generation raised in the promise of de-colonisation and we viewed it largely as a failure in India. The Chinese success with rural development held signal lessons for us. Since much has already been written about the radical movement already, all I need to add is the personal note that, unlike most others, I stayed with the study of China over the next thirty years. I did not give up my interest in Indian development either and my first project was conceived as a comparative one designed to understand why the Maoist style of peasant revolution could not occur in India.

I arrived in the US in 1976 to study Chinese history, first in Chicago where I was quickly absorbed by its famed intellectual ferment, especially developed in Indian studies. I subsequently moved with my advisor, Professor Philip Kuhn, to Harvard, where I became immersed in Harvard-style Sinology. At these institutions I learnt the all-important Sinological skills, including Japanese. I wrote a PhD at Harvard on the rural society of north China during the Japanese occupation and on the eve of the communist revolution. It was largely based on the extensive Japanese surveys and interviews—little used outside Japan—conducted in the north China plain by the research bureau of the South Manchurian Railway Company, the principal Japanese agency of colonial development and the largest research organisation in the world before the Second World War.

The materials regarding peasant life in six villages that I used were astonishingly detailed and permitted me to conduct a kind of historical ethnography of the villages. I was able to observe transformations in religious life, patterns of resource extraction, and the impact of modern institutions at the most basic level. This work was subsequently published as *Culture, Power and the State: Rural North China, 1900–1942*. Although I became increasingly absorbed by American and Japanese Sinology over the course of writing this first book, the comparison with India underlying my explorations of China has remained. Although I have conducted a few explicitly comparative studies, much more important has been the implicit comparative frame, where the knowledge of one region has been a source of questions for the other. The structure of peasant society, patterns of peasant organisation, and modes of rural penetration by urban intellectuals and activists in India continued to provide me with different perspectives from those of most others studying China. Thus it came to be that while the imagination of China had originally inspired me, in the end it was my knowledge of India that informed my understanding of China.

The comparative study of India and China has of course stimulated many European social theories, at least since Hegel. Virtually all of these studies have been designed to understand the special quality of Western modernity. Whatever the reasons for the three-pronged strategy of studying India, China and the West, it is clear that even in a sophisticated and well-informed writer like Max Weber, India and China represented a symmetrical complementarity of absences or lack in relation to the West. The excess of despotism in China and of religiosity in India meant that the rational individual or methodological individualism could not appear in those societies. The effects of these paradigmatic understandings, however, went much deeper than we often realise. These holistic and binary categories began to find their way into the study of civilisations which dominated mid-century area studies in America and elsewhere. Thus, if Louis Dumont and his American followers found religion to be the key to understanding Indian civilisation and society, Karl Wittfogel, John King Fairbank and even the great radical scholar Owen Lattimore deemed Chinese authoritarianism to be civilisationally essential.

For my part, I have found it most productive to poke around the penumbra of these large categories, in that realm of problems concealed by their great shadow. This poking around has resulted in an abiding theme that appears in my two published books and in the one that I am now completing, the theme of religion in China. The dominant Western paradigm had found religion to be less characteristic of China than of India, and the modern Chinese nationalist narrative turned this absence to be the basis of Chinese rationality. To be sure, there is no shortage of fine studies of religion in China, but for various reasons, including those shaped by these narratives, it has not been central either to the study of Chinese history or local society. One might say that it has been a relatively specialised and exotic sub-field of inquiry. My book on north Chinese villages found religious ideas and practices to be pervasive. I tried to show how, through rituals, myths, and temples, the imperial state and local society forged not a consensus, but a mode of communication which was subsequently destroyed by the modernising state—to its own great detriment. In *Rescuing History from the Nation*, my second book, one of the themes I pursued was the conflict between the modern state and popular religion. I now came to see popular religion as an inseparable and, indeed, foundational, dimension of popular culture and associational life—of an indigenous civil society, if you will—in China. I also tracked the ways in which the modern state tried to reconstitute this domain within the new categories of secularism, religion, and superstition in order to gain political ascendancy over it.

In my current work on Manchukuo, the Japanese puppet state in Manchuria during the 1930s and 1940s, I turn to the ways in which universalist ideals and practices of transcendence in popular religious societies confront modern and national visions of community and citizenship. In particular, I explore how this contest and negotiation play out in the formation of personhood. Remarkably, these religious societies which probably numbered in the thousands in the early twentieth century and commanded far greater followings than did modern, secular ones, are resurfacing in growing numbers in contemporary China. The Falungong is perhaps the most visible of these.

Fortuitously, it seems in retrospect, my intellectual journey had paralleled that of my generation of Indian historians such as Shahid Amin, Gyan Prakash, and the other Subaltern Studies scholars. They too had been immersed in peasant studies, tracking the subaltern within what Ranajit Guha described as 'the prose of counter-insurgency'. Seemingly just as fortuitous, the 'linguistic turn' hit us all at the same time. Around the time when Gayatri Spivak asked if the 'subaltern could speak', some of us in East Asian studies were reading poststructuralist literature and cultural studies. For a long time, Edward Said's *Orientalism* was our only guide to show how poststructuralism might be useful to the study of the non-West. Partha Chatterjee's 1986 study of nationalism signalled to me a move which emphasised nationalism as much as the bourgeoisie within the Subaltern Studies' critique of bourgeois nationalism.

The subsequent impact of South Asian Subaltern Studies on several areas of non-Western cultural studies and historiography in America—such as Latin America, Africa, and East Asia from the late 1980s—is worth pondering for a moment. It came at a time when South Asian studies within American academia was still in the steep decline that had been under way for almost two decades, if not more. In the early 1950s, the gap between members of the Association of Asian Studies claiming affiliation with Indian studies had not been much smaller than those claiming Chinese studies as their area of interest. It was far greater than Japanese or South East Asian studies. Already by the late 1970s, Indianists had dwindled to a few hundred, while the Sinologists had increased to over 4000 and Japanologists to almost 2000. This proportional decline has continued, although the recent numerical growth and phenomenal success of South Asians in America has probably stemmed the tide somewhat, principally by supplying a pool of ethnic students for South Asian studies classes (as also in other area studies).

Doubtless, the changing fortunes of East Asian and South Asian studies reflects the wider geopolitical situation, particularly since the American academic system is highly sensitive to the media and the economy. In this situation, the appeal of Subaltern Studies was quite remarkable. While there is no question that the high quality and creativity of the group as a whole played a major role, the Subaltern Studies group dramatised the tension being felt across several disciplines. These were disciplines such as history and historically-inspired anthropology or literary studies dominated by realist or causal epistemologies which now felt the impact of discursive and deconstructionist modes of knowing. In a symposium on Subaltern Studies organised by the American Historical Review in 1994, Florencia Mallon suggested that the ways in which the group negotiated the tension between a postmodern sensitivity to language and a Gramscian commitment to the emancipatory project was perhaps the most valuable lesson to be learnt from them.

My own *Rescuing History from the Nation* which appeared in 1995, also grappled with this question of history and discourse. I sought to explore the co-production of modern history and nationalism especially, but not exclusively, in China. I attended to the narrative structures and rhetorical strategies of a national history

and the ways it sought to appropriate the dispersed past for a progressive and enlightened national subject. In my case studies I
showed how these rhetorical structures often had significant historical effects and tried to recover dispersed histories and trace
counter-narratives of the past. Thus, for instance, the older Confu-
cian word for feudalism, *fengjian*, had contained a positive meaning in imperial Chinese society as an ideal of local autonomy direct-
ed against an aggrandising imperial power; this was transformed in
the new narrative of enlightenment history as the 'other' of modernity. Through two chapters, I track how the older narrative of
fengjian was deprived of its potential to mobilise an indigenous
critique of autocracy in the effort by dissidents to create a modern
civil society and a federated nation. In other words, I had adopted
a postcolonial perspective to understand modern discourses not
only in their own terms but as weapons in the struggle for national
modernisation.

Overtly, and in my own reckoning at the time, most of the
influences on this book derived from the scholarship on Chinese
studies, and theoretically from Western thinkers such as Walter
Benjamin and Paul Ricoeur. Yet Chinese intellectuals seem less
inclined to deconstruct their nationalism and their sense of self as
part of a Western discourse. In other words, for historical reasons
among others, the postcolonial critique does not seem relevant to
their particular situation. I had tried to argue in *Rescuing History*
that the absence of full-fledged Western colonial domination
in China—or 'imperialism without colonialism'— had obviated
the need to extirpate Western Orientalist categories on the part of
the Chinese. The ability to criticise the 'traditional' self —which
Chinese intellectuals did successfully during the May the 4th

movement (1917–21)—demands some distance from a powerful, objectifying Other. In the absence of the Other standing directly over the self, the self is able to internalise the Other in a way which appears to give it a curious autonomy from this Other. The legacy of Chinese intellectuals' inclination to target their historical culture and initiate a project of total Westernisation continues even today. Dissident Chinese intellectuals find the notion of Orientalism to be of use mainly to the PRC state which deploys it as a weapon against anti-Western imperialism from the repertoire of a nationalism that has become its most important source of legitimacy in society. Needless to say, nationalist Chinese intellectuals have no use for a methodology that seeks to deconstruct nationalist reifications during a period of nationalist glory. By and large, American studies of China is too close to the mainstream American scholarship on history and politics to even be aware of the postcolonial critique, let alone find it appealing. No matter that it is marginal and not immediately relevant to the concerns of Chinese intellectuals, I believe that the postcolonial perspective, however adapted to the circumstances, is a valuable critical position. The work of a minority of Sinologists, both American and Chinese, influenced by it can be found in the journal *Positions*.

One of the fiercest critics of postcolonialism, Arif Dirlik, is also a Chinese historian. In addition to his well-known critique, 'The Postcolonial Aura: Third World Criticism in the Age of Global Capitalism', he has recently denounced my *Rescuing History* as an expression of all that is wrong with postcolonial historical writing. I have responded to the criticisms of my work in this essay at some length elsewhere, so I will deal only with some of the broader issues he raises here. Dirlik, like Aijaz Ahmad—whose argument he follows—seeks to analyse both the identity of postcolonial scholars as well as postcolonial criticism. His analysis of the postcolonial scholar is roughly the following: these scholars are Third World intellectuals, especially from India, for whom postcolonial theory is an expression of their newly-found power in American academia. It is expressive of their power because it is not incompatible with the latest turn in global capitalism (which no longer needs Eurocentrism) and the academic system in America. Firstly, it is not at all clear that scholars identified with postcolonialism are powerful in the academic system. If it has not yet been attacked by the mainstream—as for instance has multi-culturalism—it is because it is marginal and irrelevant to it. Certainly, my personal experience indicates a much greater acceptance in the field of my earlier, mainstream social history work in Chinese studies than my later work.

Much more serious is the sociology of knowledge that Dirlik brings to bear on his analysis: that scholars have no autonomy—relative or otherwise—from their social and structural locations. This is an extraordinarily dangerous position, first because it demands a great deal of knowledge of one's colleagues' social and personal background and further assumes that it is necessary to know this in order to understand their work. A further, occupational hazard posed by it is that the same sociology requires it be applied to the Olympian practitioner. After all, Dirlik too is an immigrant scholar operating in the same commodified, transnational academic system where status, travel itineraries, and other rewards are a powerful motive for intellectual self-positioning. If we take his sociology to its logical conclusion, then all we can all do is growl from the belly of the capitalist monster. Finally, this is a sociology of knowledge that leads to the personalisation of a position, and judging from the sneering and dismissive tone he adopts towards his colleagues, there must be a pleasure to be had from it.

Surely our positions can best be understood by how the scholar envisions the relationship between her particular object of inquiry in relation to the wider structures which conditions the research object, rather than try to determine where we come from and what people there allegedly think of us. Dirlik does make an effort to study 'the identity of postcolonial criticism'. He presents two arguments: postcolonial scholarship becomes involved in the multicultural celebration of identity which does not reflect upon the structural conditions (capitalism as a totality) that engendered it. It is therefore used by capitalists and fascists for their purposes. Second, by abandoning foundationalism and the search for a subject of history, postcolonialism systematically contributes to the erasure of the revolutionary narrative and thus also ends up serving fascism and other reactionary forces.

With regard to the first point, I agree with Dirlik that all scholars, whether or not they employ the postcolonial perspective, should be more attentive to material circumstances and would urge him in this direction as well. But postcolonialism is radically different from multi-culturalism in that it is committed to the deconstruction of identity and critiques the latter's identitarian politics. It is even more particularly opposed to the reifications of national culture by fascists and other ultranationalists. Indeed, I am forced to recall an extremely unpleasant letter I received from Hindu nationalists in South Africa when I wrote an essay criticising the ascendancy of Hindu nationalism in India. With regard to Dirlik's second point, if we ignore the completely ridiculous allegation of complicity with fascism and also ignore the contradiction with his first point (multi-culturalism does require foundationalism and historical subjecthood), there is an important problem embedded in his critique. That problem is: what historical mission can guide us now that we are in a post-revolutionary situation, where, according to Dirlik himself, it is hard to return to, call for, or even desire a class-based revolution?

Whereas scholars like Aijaz Ahmad continue to insist on a return to a Marxist revolutionary view, most scholars in America including Dirlik are much less sanguine or desirous of returning to the revolutionary narrative. Indeed Dirlik's loose-cannon approach is perhaps his personal way of addressing the impasse faced by critical scholars everywhere. Critical historiography has encountered a world in which the possibilities of non-capitalist emancipation has receded and one where the revolutionary states have been discredited. At the same time, capitalist globalisation continues to widen the gap between the powerful and the powerless while the erosion of a national society itself unleashes a reaction which results in still more violent and exclusive reifications of nation, race and culture. But even if we have to wait for new theoretical clarities, there is no shortage of pressing historical problems. We certainly do not have the luxury to accuse each other of imaginary fascisms when real fascists and ultra-nationalists are busy rewriting histories that objectify nation, race and culture. There are also important issues regarding the nature of nationalism that would be worth debating widely: whether, for instance, it is uniform or multiform, what exactly changes in the history of nationalism, or how to articulate discourse analysis with that of political economy. I feel fortunate that my journey has left me with enough knowledge to know what is not acceptable, even if we can no longer dream of saving the world.

Let me close with my favorite episode from *The Journey to the West*. Seeking to discipline Sun Wukong for having played havoc at the Jade emperor's Daoist court in heaven, the Buddha held the monkey in his palm and wagered him the Jade emperor's throne if he could just jump clear off his palm. Confident in his own magical powers, Sun Wukong thought the Buddha a fool. He flew off to the pink pillars at the end of the world, pissed on one of them, somersaulted right back, and demanded the throne from the Buddha. The Buddha thundered back, 'You stinking ape. You have been on the palm of my hand the entire time.' Sure enough, the monkey smelt the stench of urine coming from the fork between the thumb and the forefinger. Just as he was about to jump off again, the Buddha tossed him out of the west gate of heaven, transformed the five fingers into the Five-phase Mountains, and pinned him down there with just enough pressure to keep him there (Wu, 1977: 173–4). If there is a saving grace in the political impasse I have outlined above, it is perhaps that all of us knowing scholars, faced with the vastness of what we may never know, might learn a little humility.

REFERENCES

Ahmad, Aijaz. 1995. 'The Politics of Literary Post-coloniality'. *Race and Class*, 36(3): 1–20.

Dirlik, Arif. 1997. 'The Postcolonial Aura: Third World Criticism in the Age of Global Capitalism'. In Arif Dirlik. Ed. *The Postcolonial Aura: Third World Criticism in the Age of Global Capitalism*. Boulder, Westview: 52–83.

———. 1999. 'How the Grinch Hijacked Radicalism: Further Thoughts on the Postcolonial'. *Postcolonial Studies*, 2(2), July: 149–63.

Duara, Prasenjit. 1991. 'The New Politics of Hinduism'. *The Wilson Quarterly*, Summer: 42–50.

————. 1993. 'The Displacement of Tension to the Tension of Displacement: Is Imperialism Still a Useful Category?'. *Radical History Review*, 57: 60–4.

————. 1995. *Rescuing History from the Nation: Questioning Narratives of Modern China*. Chicago, University of Chicago Press.

————. 1997. 'Transnationalism and the Predicament of Sovereignty: China, 1900–1945'. *American Historical Review*, Oct.: 1030–51.

————. 1998. 'Why is History Anti-theoretical?'. *Modern China*, April, 24 (2): 105–20.

————. Forthcoming. 'Leftist Criticism and the Political Impasse: Response to Arif Dirlik's "How the Grinch Hijacked Radicalism: Further Thoughts on the Postcolonial" '. *Postcolonial Studies*: 81–8.

Mallon, Florencia E. 1994. 'The Promise and Dilemma of Subaltern Studies: Perspectives from Latin American History'. *American History Review*, 99(5), Dec.: 1491–1515.

Wu, Ch'eng-en. 1977. *The Journey to the West*. Translated and edited by Anthony C Yu. Chicago, University of Chicago Press, vol. 1.

8

The Location of Scholarship

GYAN PRAKASH

What does it mean to live in the West and write about a place over which it has exercised dominance for nearly three centuries? The question becomes more complicated when one takes into account the fact that the place I write about—India—is also where I come from. There is also the fact that I write from the United States, which has few historical connections with India but exercises influence over it through its global economic, political, and ideological power. It is worth remembering, however, that the United States positions itself as a *Western* power, as a representative of the modern West. This means that, while claiming to be heir to the legacy of Western culture and power, it projects its global dominance in terms that both draw upon and go beyond the history of European colonialism. This means that, unlike Britain, where the imperial legacy overshadows scholarship on the subcontinent, what frames the study of South Asia in the United States is its status as a global power in the post-Second World War era, as the dominant representative of the West. Thus, the development of area studies programmes in the post-War era, and calls for their abandonment by powerful foundations in the post-Cold War period, can be understood in relation to the changing position of the United States as a global power.

Perhaps not surprisingly, living in the United States and writing about colonial India has made me more intimately and critically aware of the historical dominance of Western culture, knowledge, and institutions. At the same time, my appreciation of cultural difference and discrepant histories has also become sharper. By this I do not only mean the recognition and unraveling of stereotypes of East and West that clutter our lives, but also an understanding of their power—their historical sources, and what has made them so globally dominant. This is not due to the mere fact of living in the West, but living here during a time that has witnessed an enormous shift in the intellectual landscape. By this I mean the combined impact of Edward Said's insurgent critique of Orientalism, the combative scholarship produced by Subaltern Studies, new questions posed by postcolonial and feminist critics, the rethinking of Marxism triggered by political and ideological changes, Michel Foucault's genealogical accounts of Western knowledge and disciplines, and Jacques Derrida's deconstruction of Western metaphysics—all of which question established categories and assumptions. Writing in this changing scholarly milieu, I am acutely aware of the challenge to rethink South Asia in a way that acknowledges and takes into account the configuration of the modern world under Western dominance without being paralysed by this recognition.

Growing up in India, the extent to which the West was part of one's life, at least the life of the Indian middle class, was not always clear. Colonialism had institutionalised the West's dominance in the educational system. The achievement of national independence did not decolonise colonial education; instead, it universalised the West even more. The cultural authority of Western science and rationality—told in triumphal stories about Copernicus and the epochal clash between the Church's medievalism and the scientific revolution—were drilled into us. I am often told now that this is not the 'real' history of the West, but somehow colonial education failed to qualify its stories about Europe: outside its borders, Europe lives and universalises itself in mythic images. So much so that this mythical history does not even care to mark itself as a provincial story but represents itself as a universal narrative of progress. That is how we were taught. The West was History, and Indians became a part on Western terms. One studied the histories of Britain and Europe to identify the emergence and crystallisation of universals—humanism, democracy, the rule of reason, science, and modernity. India's history was plotted alongside and against this universal pattern to reveal both its 'lacks' and its positive contribution to History. The only discordant note was struck by the intrusion of British colonialism in India's history, but the account of Indian nationalism's eventual triumph helped to maintain the master narrative. Colonialism was a terrible thing, but Bacon and Shakespeare were of universal significance. So internalised was the

117

West in our education that we not only learnt it well, we made it our own.

Marxism was not free from the representation of the West as History, but it offered a critical vantage point. It taught us that our bourgeoisie's anti-imperialism was compromised by its commitment to fatten the capitalist and landed classes at the expense of working classes and the peasantry. Such a conception animated my first foray into academic research. I began working on the history of bonded labour in India in order to both expose the ideological pretensions of the state and understand the class forces that sustained unfree production relations. I remember closely following the debate among Indian Marxists on the question of capitalism in agriculture in the pages of the *Economic and Political Weekly* during the early 1970s. While some argued that Indian agriculture was capitalist, others asserted that production relations in the countryside remained semi-feudal in character. Reports and surveys on the existence of bonded labour confirmed the impression that at the very least India's capitalism differed greatly from the classic British pattern analysed by Marx. I went to Lenin's writings on Russian agriculture and Karl Kautsky's study on the capitalist transformation of German agriculture to get a better theoretical grasp of the Indian experience. European feudalism and its transition to capitalism also appeared relevant. I scoured library shelves in New Delhi for books and articles on feudal relations in different parts of Europe. My friends and I eagerly circulated and read with a great sense of expectancy articles by European scholars, gallantly translated by sympathetic students in foreign languages department, barely legible on coarse, yellowing pages, and hailed as breakthroughs which, needless to say, never happened. Though I

118

learned a great deal from all this feverish reading, I soon tired of trying to read Indian history through Europe and began to look at the literature on the Third World. French debates on the slave mode of production in Africa and Latin American writings on dependent development consumed my interest. Above all, I became intrigued by anthropology because it seemed to call into question the Eurocentric universalism of history.

My interest in anthropology drew me to the United States because I knew that its graduate programmes were flexible and permitted one to do interdisciplinary work. So, I joined the University of Pennsylvania in 1979 ready to study anthropology systematically, while pursuing a history degree. This was very refreshing. But I also found the influence of Indology—or what we soon started calling Orientalism after reading Edward Said's work—on South Asian studies to be stifling. I did not take well to the conservatism of Indology and South Asian studies. I do not mean just the political conservatism of area studies but also its intellectual style and tenor. It seemed like a closed discipline, a guild with austere conventions and rigid rules. I valued the systematic training that I received by reading classic works in different disciplines concerned with South Asia. But the whole area studies approach seemed too stiff, too confident in its ability to define what constituted South Asia. Ironically, it was the formal study of anthropology that I had eagerly sought which made me realise how important disciplinary procedures and approaches were in defining South Asia; if Indian society were to be understood through the work of symbols, this was in no small part due to the fact that students trained in symbolic anthropology went out looking for the play of symbols. This is not to say that symbolic anthropology was wrong, but only that the desire to study symbols was generated by the discipline itself. Later, I came to understand the politics of such disciplinary practices, but at that time I saw them as too academic, too distant from the political concerns that had drawn me to the study of bonded labour.

There was another way in which I found the study of South Asia too wrapped up with itself. This happened when I noticed that, sometimes, my American colleagues in South Asian studies saw me through the lens of their disciplinary training, through what they had learned about Hinduism, caste, kinship, and regions. It was disconcerting to be viewed as an object of knowledge, though it did not occur to me to ask how I had come to occupy such a position or what enabled me to resist it. To be viewed via the media of academic concepts, however, was frustrating because I felt close to Western cultural forms—popular music, cinema, literature, philosophy. My American colleagues in the South Asian field were often taken aback by my familiarity with 'their' culture, unprepared as they were to encounter the object of their study so close to home and talking back in their own language. I think most of them ended up seeing me as an anomaly, an exception to an India that remained in their minds as decidedly religious, caste-bound, Sanskritic, and traditional. But this whole experience also made me reflect on the difference of my 'Western' experience—on how ineluctably Indian was my westernisation.

My American training did not steer me away from defining my research topic in relation to Indian political concerns. I returned to the history of bonded labour in Bihar as the topic of my dissertation research. I had already done some archival work on this subject before I came to the United States, but now I had a more finished project which included a combination of archival work and anthropological field research. During the course of the research I became aware that the question of labour bondage could not be understood as a feudal relic that had somehow managed to live beyond its time into modernity. It was part and parcel of India's modern history, though it could not be understood simply as a product of the state-supported power of landlords and usurers. When I told friends and acquaintances in India the topic of my research, they would ask incredulously: 'Are they still bonded?' Clearly, almost everyone, including left-wing critics of the state, thought that bondage belonged to another time, that it had no place in modern life. I did not turn around and ask why they should suppose that it should have ended long ago, for I, too, shared their view. Though I was beginning to have doubts about the premises of such a question, these were vague rumblings of discomfort, not a clearly articulated understanding.

After I completed my dissertation and sat down to write it into a book, I decided to tackle questions that had baffled me head-on. What are the historical origins of the assumption that freedom is a natural human condition, and labour bondage a suppression of that supposed innate state? How was it that such an assumption became instituted in India's history? As I sought to answer these questions, it became clear to me that the discourse of freedom functioned much like what Foucault describes as the 'repressive hypothesis'. Just as the discourse of sexual repression institutes sex as a natural instinct which is repressed subsequently by social institutions and unshackled by psychotherapy, the concept of freedom projects labour bondage as the suppression of free labour imposed by backward and feudal ideologies and institutions which need to be overthrown in order to set society on its natural course. If one were to ask how such a discourse became dominant in Indian history, the answer would lie in colonialism. It was British rule, I argued, that institutionalised the discourse of freedom as an aspect of imperial domination. In this process, it had recast a range of dependent social ties, representing and acting upon them in terms of capitalist categories. In short, the question of bonded labour in India was inseparable from the exercise of colonial power and its forms of knowledge.

It was in the process of identifying the colonial genealogy of the issue of bonded labour and in trying to outline another form of historical representation that I came upon Subaltern Studies. This is not the place to recount the achievements of this scholarship except to note that I found its effort to outline alternatives to dominant historical representations paralleled my own. More generally, the writings of Ranajit Guha and others in the group stimulated my interest in tracing connections between élitist historiography and the history of the production of Western knowledge about South Asia. As I wrote articles on historiography, the central question that preoccupied me was: How does one make languages associated with élitist and Western domination speak in other tongues? How do we critique positions that we also inhabit? Another way of describing this concern is to ask that, given that the West is everywhere (as Ashis Nandy has suggested), how does one find other ways of knowing and being? It is in this context that I have found Homi Bhabha's writings on hybridity enormously enabling. In my reading, his concept of hybridity does not celebrate the misrule of mixture against the rule of identity; rather, hybridity emerges as a time of in-betweenness, as a place of tension, of irreconcilable contradictions between unequal and incommensurate positions of power/knowledge which can serve as sites for altering conditions of domination. I have found this approach useful in my recent work on the functioning of science as a metaphor of modernity in India, arguing that the very utilisation of science as an instrument of alien rule created conditions also for its repositioning.

Elsewhere, I have spoken of the desire to chart subaltern sites of knowledge as a form of postcolonial criticism, that is, as an attempt to identify pasts and positions that remain at odds with those that were instituted and authorised by colonialist and nationalist élites. This is not without risks. There is no denying that the glossing of studies dealing with a wide range of places and times as postcolonial ends up making their difference from the West their defining feature. This plays into the representation of a range of histories as varied forms of the Other, confirming the West's dominance. Having said this, it is equally necessary to recognise that one cannot simply wish away the history of the last four centuries; the project to write about other places in their own terms has to include deconstructive readings of Western power and knowledge. Perhaps this imperative has less force in India itself, where the Western legacy operates through national institutions, where Orientalist representations, the domineering logic of modernity, and capitalist exploitation are experienced as aspects of indigenous power. There, critical scholarship is understandably concerned less with the continuing influence of Western knowledge and more with its use by the Hindu right-wing and the state. In the United States, on the other hand, the demands of criticism require a focus on ways in which the knowledge of other places and other times serves Western power. It is for this reason that postcolonial scholarship in the West engages with the colonial and imperial genealogies of the histories of non-Western regions. This does not mean an acceptance of the East–West dichotomy but a recognition of its historical force in structuring both dominant and dominated societies. Thus, postcolonial scholarship has produced accounts that suggest that colonialism not only reconstituted the culture and society of the colonies but also those of the metropole.

Some misunderstand this imperative altogether and view the critique of Western power and knowledge as a postmodernist ideological manoeuvre of USA-centred capitalism. Worse still, it is viewed as a reach for power by the élites of Third World origins located in the United States. It is argued that the critique of Orientalist representations and colonial power conceals the role of the real culprit—capitalism—which underlies inequality and exploitation, and helps the attempt to remake the world according to the ideology of multiculturalism and identity politics. Strangely enough, those who make location into a fetish seldom stop to ana-lyse their own. Somehow, the intellectual air emanating out of the late-imperial gothic of Oxbridge suffers from no locational miasma. The gravitational charge of location also vanishes miraculously if one moves to the East after living and working for decades in the West. I suspect that the *ressentiment* underlying this locationism manifests anxieties produced by profound changes in how we understand the location of criticism. It used to be the case that criticism was clearly and firmly identified with certain institutions, subjects, and locations associated with Enlightenment rationality. As this has come under deep suspicion, it has also produced the anxiety that the irrational passions of race, tribe, and culture cloud the clear Enlightenment vision of universal reason.

The Location of Scholarship

As I see it, my location in the United States and the nature of my work form part of the unsettling of the ground we stand upon. I do not find this disorienting or disabling. On the contrary, I believe that the unfixing of India from its Orientalist, colonialist, and nationalist moorings has been salutary, for it has permitted explorations of histories and knowledges that these frameworks did not allow. It has also permitted alternative ways of exploring commonalities and differences with histories of other regions of the world. What are the terms in which we can relate with, for example, the Latin American experiences, if we are to dispense with categories authorised by colonial domination and neocolonialism? How are we to understand and learn from the study of Africa if we no longer adopt the area studies framework? Such questions and dialogues have become possible because of a shift in the academic authority away from traditional centres and the emergence of new locations of scholarship. This, too, is part of the loss of old certainties about knowledge and reflects the increasing attention we pay now to the question of its location. But location not in the sense that the nature of scholarship can be read off easily from the physical location of its production, but that it is always situated in a complex web of history, power, and culture. Seen this way, the opening up of new avenues and kinds of scholarship should be understood as efforts to produce knowledge with a fuller recognition of its relationship with power and with a desire to act upon it. For me, this means seeking a scholarship that resists dominant ways of representing India both in the West and in India itself.

As my inquiry into what sustains inequality and exploitation in South Asia has developed into a critique of the modern West, it has dissolved the ontological East/West opposition. The East is nothing but the West's distorted self-image. Yet, this opposition has dominated the modern history of (and knowledge about) South Asia. My scholarship is poised in-between the recognition of these two lives of the East and West; it is there that I locate possibilities of new kinds of knowledge about South Asia.

9

Globalisation, Democratisation and the Evacuation of History?*

DIPESH CHAKRABARTY

I begin from the observation/assumption that debates that arose in the 1980s in the wake of Edward Said's *Orientalism* have now been somewhat superseded by questions to do with the cultural politics of globalisation. This does not mean that problems of Eurocentrism in the human sciences have been successfully resolved. Far from it. My book *Provincialising Europe* is devoted to discussing the problems of interpreting Indian history through categories derived from, or closely allied to, modern political philosophy. I argued that these categories, in spite of their global relevance and even origins, have never quite transcended the peculiarities of European histories within which they were initially conceived.[1] However, the East/West question, I now feel, is cut athwart today by the forces of globalisation and mass-democracy. In what follows, I briefly explain that proposition with respect to my own discipline, History, and discuss some of the dilemmas it faces today precisely because of demands for democratisation of knowledge. These demands arise as social groups, once marginal and subordinated, become powerful actors in the political arena. The so-called Dalits (the ex-Untouchables and other low-caste groups similarly oppressed) of India are a case in point. Over the last couple of decades, Indian electoral processes and policies of affirmative action have produced some powerful leaders from the Dalit and low-caste communities at many different levels of public-political life in the country. There has been a direct impact of this development on the politics of historiography in India. Radical histories, it is now assumed by many, must address historiographical problems from Dalit perspectives. Indeed, it was the criticism that *Subaltern Studies* had never included a Dalit voice that led the editors of volume 9 of the series to invite an essay by Kancha Illaih the pre-eminent Dalit intellectual of India.[2] My own intellectual trajectory is tied up with this question of the relationship between democracy and its impact on knowledge formations. I have to clarify, however, that the argument I put forward here remains as yet, in many ways, an Indian argument. My examples are Indian and the democracy I have in mind in the Indian one. The task of working out the larger ramifications of my argument will have to wait for another occasion.

Europeans invented a form of knowledge in the late eighteenth century that for a long time occupied a position of prestige in Indian, and particularly Bengali, thought of the late nineteenth and twentieth centuries. This was the new discipline of History. Muslim rulers had brought certain traditions of history-writing to India and added them to other traditions of chronicling that existed in the country. But what the Europeans brought was different and new. Sometimes false nationalism or false internationalism make people claim that non-Westerners had their versions of what Europeans regarded as history. I think that that simply overstates the case. It is true that the modern academic knowledge-form called history has never had a fixed and unchanging form. History, the discipline, changes through debates and innovations among historians. What the Europeans brought to India may be broadly termed 'historicism'. Again, historicism itself is a problematic word, given to many meanings.[3] What I mean is this. History as a developmental story, as an explanation of how things came to be the way they were in the present, history as a story of human action devoid altogether of divine intervention, history as a process of change both illustrating and subject to sociological laws—all this was new and came to Indians as a result of British rule. Indian intellectuals did not take to the new idea of history overnight, though the idea was appreciated quite early in the nineteenth century. For Bengal, the part of India I am from, it can be safely stated that between the 1870s and the 1910s, Bengali intellectuals, young and old, got involved in vigorous debates about the idea of historical evidence, about what could properly constitute 'proof' of historical truths. Central to this debate were the ideas of 'truth' and 'reality'. A certain kind of realism won the day. It was not only debates among historians that helped to create an investment—for literate Bengalis in general—in realist modes of narration. It was also a result of the interest that the Bengali intelligentsia took in the colonial law-courts and their proceedings. Gautam Bhadra, one of my colleagues in the *Subaltern Studies* group, has just completed a book manuscript on an interesting case of impersonation that happened in Bengal in the first half of the nineteenth century and that was followed by a prolonged court case. Examining a well-known account of this story that was written in the 1870s, Bhadra demonstrates the degree to which British efforts to establish 'laws of evidence' suitable for India absorbed intellectuals in nineteenth-century Bengal.[4] If we looked forward from this period, the 1870s, on to the twentieth century, the march of the discipline of history would seem unstoppable. The Indian Historical Records Commission, with an assigned mission to collect, catalogue, and preserve historical documents, was set up in 1918, thanks in part to the untiring efforts of pioneering historians such as Sir Jadunath Sarkar. The History Indian Congress, a professional body of teachers and researchers of history, was established in the mid-1930s. History, as a discipline, rose even further in prominence after independence. The Government of India founded two premier business schools in the 1960s—the Indian Institutes of Management at Ahmedabad and Calcutta—both of which made history into a compulsory subject for prospective managers, something that would sound like an absurdity to any business school today. Mrs Gandhi's education minister in the 1970s, Professor Nurul Hasan, was a historian who helped found the Indian Council of Historical Research. Indeed, History, one might say, even vied with economics in the 1970s for the position of the most prestigious social science in India.[5]

There were, of course, very important changes that History as a discipline had undergone in India in the period between, say, the early Indian debates about historical truth in the 1910s and the prominence that the discipline achieved in the 1970s and 1980s. The old debates were part of anti-colonial nationalism, and were not marked by any particular political ideology beyond that of nationalism itself. Historical researchers were intensely interested in finding out about Indian imperial traditions, traditions of self-rule and democratic or republican governance, about literary, cultural and aesthetic inheritance, about instances of nation-building and statesmanship in ancient and pre-British India, and so on. Obviously, their agenda was nationalist. But these early pioneers of modern historiography busied themselves with discovering sources and with filling gaps in—or correcting—contemporary knowledge of the past. There were personal rivalries and varying ethical standards between these historians, but together they established the importance of the cultural artefact called 'historical evidence'. If there were no credible historical evidence, this generation said in effect, then there was no history.

History as a discipline has remained anchored in this idea of evidence. But there have been some very significant changes in the world of historical scholarship in India since independence. Indian scholars who did their PhDs in Oxford or Cambridge (or in Delhi, Aligarh and Calcutta) in the 1950s and 1960s, found themselves in a situation in which History, the discipline, increasingly fell under the spell of varieties of Marxism. Post-colonial nationalism, with its official insistence on planned economy and industrialisation, on non-alignment and eventual diplomatic and cultural friendship with the Soviet Union, Mrs Gandhi's populist programme of 'eradicating poverty'—all created a setting in which a certain kind of Marxist historiography flourished under official patronage. The Indian Council of Historical Research became a funding body controlled by Marxist historians close to the government. These developments in turn led to some significant institutional changes—the prestigious Centre of Historical Studies at the Jawaharlal Nehru University, Delhi, or the Centre for Studies in Social Science, Calcutta, for instance, were direct results of this new influence of Marxism over the social sciences in India. But equally significant, though less commented on, were some silent and subtle changes that affected the way historians came to relate to the knowledge they produced. A scholar such as Sir Jadunath Sarkar (1870–1958) believed that the condition for writing 'true' histories was an unflinching and ethical devotion to truth on the historian's part. Not every historian could live up to Sir Jadunath's standards in these matters but his pursuit of a fiercely non-partisan attachment to 'truth' perhaps remained the ideal for most historians of his generation.[6] Marxist historians of the 1970s, on the other hand, came to see truth itself as partisan, as something totally caught up in the battle between classes and their interests, battles that were supposed to constitute society. Truth or knowledge now figured as representations of interest. Indeed so deep was the investment this generation of Marxist Indian historians had made in the patronage they received from the government that one of them actually wrote, once, that the condition for telling the truth in history was financial patronage from the state. Private money, this historian assumed, could only speak for private interest. His further Hegelian assumption was that the state spoke for everybody, so it was all right to be on the payroll of the state. I do not name this historian because it is not my purpose to isolate any individuals. This historian simply expressed a shared attitude of his generation.

I have a direct, personal relationship to this history. After my undergraduate degree (which was in science) from the University of Calcutta, I went to do an MBA from the Indian Institute of Management, Calcutta. And that was where I encountered History, and a Marxist version at that. For the syllabus-makers of this institution had decided that while future managers needed to know capitalist economics, their memories must be anti-colonial. Hence they must know something about how India was bled by British colonial exploitation. The compulsory course in history was called 'Economic Backwardness in Historical Perspective'. Our professor, a charismatic teacher who actually inspired me to be a historian and who personally aided my academic growth, asked why India was poor and put the blame squarely on colonial exploitation. He was not alone in holding that view. That opinion rang through Indian historiography of the 1970s like a chorus line. And it gave history, the discipline, an immediate sense of political relevance. You could not explain modern India without discussing the deleterious impact of colonial economic exploitation. Unlike the generation of Jadunath Sarkar, who thought 'bias' was something the historian strived to overcome within himself or herself, we followed E.H. Carr in assuming that history was inevitably partisan. All one could do was to proclaim one's bias, and proudly, so that the bias was seen as working in favour of the oppressed and the exploited. In other words, by the time my generation of historians found themselves inhabiting the social science world of India, the air was heavy with ideologies. And knowledge, we assumed, was always a weapon in ideological battles.

But the weapon still had a character that made it recognisable as 'knowledge' belonging to the discipline of history. True, this knowledge was now to be placed in the service of fights for social justice, democracy and equality, but a Jadunath Sarkar would have still recognised the methods of research we pursued. These methods still needed training. One had to go to universities, learn to distinguish judiciously between different kinds of evidence, judge what was admissible and what was inadmissible as evidence, read and write for professional journals, present papers at conferences, face professional criticism, and so on. Doing a PhD was one simple way of doing this. Even when we in *Subaltern Studies* rebelled in the 1980s against nationalist histories that were élitist, this consensus about methods of research remained intact.[7] It was not difficult for scholars who disagreed with us on questions of points of view to praise good research when they found it in the pages of *Subaltern Studies*. This is why early *Subaltern Studies* did not threaten the discipline of history. History was based on certain universally acceptable rules of evidence. These rules gave a disciplinary unity to history and made it possible for the discipline to contain and represent many different points of view. Our research methods carried the stamp of the very particular kind of training and higher education we had received. For example, in the 1980s, the Hindu extremists laid claim to a mosque on the ground that it was built by destroying a Hindu temple that stood on the birthplace of the mythical god-king Rama. Unsurprisingly, secular and left-minded historians at the prestigious Jawaharlal Nehru University (JNU) in New Delhi brought out a collection of essays that sought to educate the general citizen-reader on the fundamental distinction between historical truths and myths.[8] The distinction turned on the question of evidence. The JNU historians were not naïve in any sense. They would not have been surprised to be told, for example, that written histories could also peddle myths of one kind or another. But they would have still insisted, with good reason, that professional history-writing depends on the existence of public and verifiable pieces of evidence. One cannot produce evidence with respect to births and deaths of gods and god-kings. This particular example is not meant as a criticism of my professional colleagues in Delhi. Nor do I mean to approve of the politics that led eventually to the vandalisation of a historical and religious building. I want to raise a question about the relation between a social-science discipline such as history and the resolution of conflicts in public life that raised questions about the past.

The intervention by the left-secular historians of Delhi in the debates around the Hindu extremists' programme of destroying the mosque in Ayodhya was an attempt to use the disciplinary authority of History to help settle a controversy raging both inside and outside the academy. Developments in Indian democracy, however, have increasingly drawn a question mark over the capacity of the discipline of history to adjudicate in disputations in public life about questions of the past. For instance, the distinction between a myth and verifiable historical fact may seem obvious to professional historians. But there is nothing natural or god-given to this distinction. Being able to make such a distinction calls for training in particular ways of reasoning. These modes of reasoning are not necessarily obvious to citizens from the subaltern classes that now actively shape the character of Indian democracy. For you have to be a certain kind of literate and educated person even to be interested in any abstract formulation of the distinction between myth and history. A peasant-citizen of India may indeed make use of 'historical facts' to contest 'myths' or vice versa but he or she would be doing so in particular situations. The abstract and general distinction between the two may not be of any interest to him or her in ways that are independent of contexts. Yet the JNU historians obviously believed that educating the public in certain routine and abstract distinctions made in the class room could help solve a dispute in Indian national life that had a bearing on questions of the past.

This particular example of the relationship between academic knowledge and public life points to a situation peculiar to Indian democracy though the ramifications of what I have to say may go beyond India. If we assume that the role of the university and its various disciplines are to give citizens the skills and knowledge they need in order for them to become proper citizens, we make a connection between citizenship and formal education. Indeed, this could be one way of democratising knowledge, i.e. by making it available to all. With respect to the subaltern classes, this view in effect says: let the peasant go to schools and universities and imbibe the consciousness and reasoning that are displayed in the methods of academic thinking. The critical question here is that of the potential citizen imbibing particular ways of reasoning. This reasoning is embodied not so much in the factual content of the various disciplines, as in their methods. Hence the emphasis our JNU historians placed on questions of proof, evidence, and the archives, as they weighed into a public debate. The idea surely was to make

136

the 'masses' or the public learn the historian's method of reasoning. But to adopt this position in the politics of democratising knowledge would also be to visualise a democracy that, fundamentally, asked the subaltern of today to wait until s/he acquired the educational training that would equip him/her for citizenly action. This gesture has a certain kind of élitism built into it even if a benevolent élite saw itself in the role of being custodians for a people and/or a nation. The attitude is élitist in that it temporises on the question of democracy. The position is somewhat like that of a John Stuart Mill on self-rule by Indians or Africans. The latter, in Mill's argumentation, were never quite ready for self-rule, thus necessitating the role of the self-appointed colonial powers. In *Provincialising Europe*, I referred to this gesture as symptomatic of the 'not yet' structure of the historicist conception of time. Colonial rule was predicated on such a 'not yet' gesture that allowed Europeans to tell Indians to wait for self-rule until they were ready to do so. This structure and its attendant policies and politics exist in postcolonial India. But what was truly revolutionary about the Indian decision to go in for universal adult franchise after Independence was that it fundamentally repudiated this paternalist understanding of democracy. Indian democrats, at least in this move, replaced the 'not yet' gesture of colonial rule by the democratic temporal horizon of the 'now'. By this single move was inaugurated the time of mass democracy in India. The peasant and members of other subaltern classes in India were made citizens overnight without having to wait for formal training in the doctrinal or procedural sides of citizenship.[9] In the context of our present discussion, the question then boils down to this. What is the relationship between

democracy and the functioning of knowledge in the human sciences? How does the advent of 'mass' forms of democracy make a
differ-ence to this relationship?

A sentence in Foucault's *Discipline and Punish* helps us to
think through this question. Foucault writes: 'the first of the great
operations of discipline is . . . [to] transform the confused, useless
or dangerous multitudes into ordered multiplicities.'[10] Foucault
helps us to think about the limits to disciplinary formations. These
limits are constituted by 'the multitudes' who, from disciplinary
perspectives, appear 'dangerous and confusing'. In other words,
the very idea of discipline, Foucault says, is wedded to the task of
managing diversity and heterogeneity. If disciplines (in the many
different senses in which Foucault used the term, ranging from
procedures of governmentality to the formation of normalising
knowledge-systems) aid in producing 'organised multiplicities,'
then the organisation of such multiplicities must be achieved along
some axes of sameness. The scales or units by which such multiplicities are organised would precisely refer to that which was shared between things otherwise plural and different. A classificatory
system, for example. In the context of a democracy, the organisers
of such multiplicities—people who visualised or conceptualised
the organisation—would then be the governing élite (or class) in
an (often self-appointed) role of managing a democracy on behalf
of others. Academics may not look like they have anything to do
with managerial functions. But it does not take much thinking
to see that one function of tertiary education is to fit people out
for modern bureaucracies. Academic training is not all about learning to appreciate reason in some pure form. Examinations, having
to engage with the genres of essays, precis, projects and so on also
give us training in skills that are essential to the process Foucault

once called 'governmentality'.[11] Disciplines, according to Foucault, cannot be separated from the business of government and administration of lives and prosperity under modern institutions. In that sense, disciplines cannot be separated from an élitist construction of politics.

From nationalist historians such as Sir Jadunath Sarkar to the more democratically minded Marxist historians of the 1970s, the commitment to preserve the core rationality of a *discipline* of thought called 'history' was a commitment to a particular idea of democracy. This was a vision of democracy that saw itself as never fully functioning until everybody had received a degree of formal training in the arts of reasoning in the human sciences. Politics is here fundamentally a structure of pedagogy. But it is a particular structure. Pedagogy here is understood as the same as what is practised in the institutions of higher learning. Disciplines arise as part of such a pedagogical understanding of politics.

But alongside this kind of politics, there exist—perhaps increasingly—another practice of politics in mass-democracies. We could, following Foucault, call it 'the politics of the multitude'.[12] Politics on this register is not an experience of pedagogy as it is ideally associated with the university. To be human, it is assumed in this new understanding of politics, is not only to have the *capacity* to be political; it *is* to be political. The capacity is always there in a realised form, whether one is formally educated or not. This thought has been with us for the last few decades in many different forms—in extensions of voting and civil rights, for instance, to Aboriginals in Australia or to African-Americans in the United States in the 1960s. (It always marked a departure from the demand 'let them be educated first . . .'). It was also there in the feminist slogan, 'the personal is political' (though sometimes the

139

expression of this took pedagogical forms in consciousness-raising groups). The politics of the multitude can be fundamentally opposed to the disciplinary rationality of disciplines even when it pays lip service to such disciplines or uses them simply as a legitimising device or in a spirit of pragmatism.

We have already encountered a version of this new political vision in the pages of *Subaltern Studies*. In the essay he wrote for volume 9 of *Subaltern Studies*, Kancha Illaih deliberately set aside all academic procedures to claim for the Dalitbahujan peoples a past that would not necessarily be vindicated by the methodological protocols of the historian or the textual analyst. The word 'Dalitbahujan' signifies solidarity between Dalits, ex-Untouchables, and other groups of lower-caste backgrounds, *bahujan* literally meaning a majority. Illaih's radical claim was that the existing archives and ways of reading them—the discipline of history, to be precise—have to be rejected if the Dalitbahujans are to find pasts that help them in their present struggles.[13] He stated:

> The methodology and epistemology that I use in this essay being what they are, the discussion might appear 'unbelievable', 'unacceptable', or 'untruthful' to those 'scholars and thinkers' who are born and brought up in Hindu families. Further, I deliberately do not want to take precautions, qualify my statements, footnote my material, nuance my claims, for the simple reason that my statements are not meant to be nuanced in the first place. They are meant to raise Dalitbahujan consciousness. . . .[14]

There is obviously a vision here—howsoever inchoate but a vision nevertheless—of a modern and democratic politics that does not connect itself, except pragmatically, to social-science or humanistic disciplines and that in fact may actually entail their repudiation.

Illaih has his own ideas about pedagogy and consciousness-raising but they are not tied to the pedagogic principles of the university. I still remember the debate among the editorial members of *Subaltern Studies* that preceded our decision to publish this essay that deliberately—and as a political decision—flouted all the methodological principles that constituted the discipline of history. But how could one have an interest in subaltern politics and not respect the gesture of rejection of academic discipline that was an inherent part of Ilaih's vision of the political?[15]

A similar rejection of the historian's history is recorded in Badri Narayan's recent study of 'Dalit political discourse' in the Uttar Pradesh region.[16] In a chapter on the histories that the Dalits themselves are producing, Narayan helps us see that these histories are not any less 'mythical' than those produced by the Hindu right, except, of course, their political aims are very different. They aim to give the oppressed groups of Indian society pride in their identities and in their pasts, and to prepare them for their struggles of the present. Narayan calls these histories written by the Dalits themselves 'mythhistory of Dalits'. He says that these histories 'claim to be different from the previous histories . . . [they] never draw on the thoughts of Ambedkar, or on Marxism or any alternative historical paradigm'.[17] They are made up of 'mythical' and 'folk' elements and speak of the 'glories' of particular castes.[18] These written and widely circulated histories are part of the print culture no doubt and play a pedagogical role in Indian politics but it is clear that they would be as defiant of the historian's understanding of 'evidence' and 'proof' as would be the Hindu extremists' claims on the past.

If these Dalit histories are evidence of challenges posed to disciplines such as history by the advent of mass democracy, the impact of globalisation becomes evident from another recent attempt by Dalit intellectuals to re-read the past. Quite a few Indian Dalit intellectuals have argued very recently—and some of them took the argument to the UN-sponsored conference on racism in Durban that was held a few months ago—that caste oppression is not historically specific to India, that it is the same as racist discrimination. Some well-known Indian sociologists, otherwise devoted to both democracy as well as the methodological strictures of their disciplines, have demurred; some actually have audibly disagreed.[19] But it is clear that while mobilising under global banner of 'race' may evacuate Indian history of all its specificity and thus upset the professional historian or the anthropologist, there are enormous and immediate political gains to be made by the downtrodden by globalising their issues. They will thus create one, a more or less homogeneous, history for the world's oppressed. Marxism once tried to give the world's working people the same history. But the effort never challenged the élitism of 'ordered multiplicities' represented by the disciplines of knowledge. The new claims to a global, homogeneous past for the oppressed is fundamentally different in that they do not look to the theory-classes of the university to provide them with evidence, proof and justificatory argumentation. They emanate out of the politics of the multitude and the multitude can, if need be, argue in ways that bypass the methods of abstraction and reasoning one learns by going to schools, colleges and universities.

Needless to say, I am discussing a tendency that has become increasingly powerful and visible, but it remains a tendency nevertheless. I am not describing a wholesale transition that has already taken place. The vision of politics that needs the rationality of academic disciplines to create 'ordered multiplicities' out of the 'dangerous multitudes' now exists side by side with what I have called, following Foucault and with a nod in the direction of Hardt and Negri, 'the politics of the multitude'. This is not a simple conflict between a 'politics of recognition' and a 'methodology of knowledge'. The methodologies of knowledge were never, in the first place, neutral to the politics of recognition. How would they otherwise help in the construction of 'ordered multiplicities' that were, after all, identities (such as nations, classes, castes, races, etc.) and hence subject to the politics of recognition? Intellectuals such as Illaih are trying to open up another space for the politics of recognition that is not dependent on the rationality of academic disciplines. In the age of mass forms of democracy, the politics of the latter kind are not a passing phenomenon. What does a professional historian, a *Subaltern Studies* historian at that, do, faced with the challenges to the discipline thrown up by the subaltern-citizen of a mass democracy every day? The option of withdrawing back into the citadels of the discipline and chiding mythmakers of both the left and the right for violating historical truths will only isolate the discipline from the turmoil of public life. It will turn history into a merely academic-aesthetic enterprise. Only professional historians will, in that case, read each other for the aesthetic pleasure of reading 'good' histories. Yet one cannot forget all the training one has received in becoming a historian and say, after some vulgar and rightly discredited positions in postmodernist discussions, that there is nothing called 'fact' and that the difference between 'facts' and unverifiable 'myths' has ceased to matter. It matters because the politics of 'organised multiplicities' exist alongside, and intertwined with, the politics of the multitude.

However, the coming of the latter vision of the political marks a real change in the history of democracy. There is no point lamenting, in the manner of a B.K. Nehru, that India made a mistake adopting universal suffrage so early in its republican career when her people 'had had little opportunity of developing an ethos of self-governance.'[20] Fear of 'the masses' is no longer a productive option in Indian public life. B.K. Nehru's fears can at most be respected as the private fears of a citizen. The politics of the multitude are here to stay. The only viable option, it seems to me, for academic-intellectuals wedded to the disciplinary protocols of their human sciences, is to engage in a conversation with the subaltern-citizen to see how and what ways these protocols may indeed serve, even today, entrenched privilege in society. Only by subjecting themselves to such a process will the humanist disciplines such as history be able to further democratise their methods of knowledge. It is difficult to know the future in advance but contemporary debates in history departments about history and memory, history and the media, or about history and myth, are ripple-effects produced by larger changes in the functioning of democratic societies. Historians are sometimes advised to continue to be historians on a 'business as usual' basis. Debates about methodologies or questions about history's epistemology are sometimes frowned upon and dismissed as 'passing fads' of the day. One thing, however, is clear at least to me: that to ignore these debates is to remain blind to the evolving relationship between disciplines and democracy. Hence the need for a critical examination of the basic presuppositions of our discipline at the same time as we engage public life as practitioners of these disciplines. It is not surprising therefore that *Subaltern Studies*, which began as some version of 'history from below', should have by now produced critiques of history as well.

NOTES

*Thanks are due to Veronique Bénéï and Jackie Assayag for comments on an earlier draft.

1. *Provincialising Europe: Postcolonial Thought and Historical Difference* (Princeton, New Jersey: Princeton University Press, 2000).
2. See Kancha Illaih, 'Productive Labour, Consciousness and History: The Dalitbahujan Alternative', in Shahid Amin and Dipesh Chakrabarty, eds, *Subaltern Studies IX: Writings on South Asian History and Society* (Delhi: Oxford University Press, 1996), pp. 165–200. Ilaih began by saying: 'Mainstream historiography has done nothing to incorporate the Dalitbahujan perspective in the writing of Indian history: *Subaltern Studies* is no exception to this'.
3. See *Provincialising Europe*, Introduction and Chapter 1.
4. Gautam Bhadra, *Jaal Raajaar Golpo* (in Bengali) [The Story of a Fake King] (Kolkata: Ananda Publishers, forthcoming).
5. The Indian Council of Historical Research has been subject to contrary political pulls in different periods of its existence. When it was formed, the Council was controlled mainly by historians attuned to the causes of the left. As a right-wing Hindu political party came to power in the late 1980s and the 1990s, there have been attempts to give history-writing in India an aggressively Hindu colour, a tendency sometimes referred to attempts to 'saffronise' textbooks and histories.
6. See the discussion in H. R. Gupta, *Life and Letters of Sir Jadunath Sarkar* (Hoshiarpur: Punjab University, 1958).
7. I should point out here that *Subaltern Studies* began as an intervention in the field of Indian history. Contributions to the first three volumes drew on Anthropology and Economics but the debates that Subaltern

145

Studies addressed initially were predominantly located in the discipline of history.

8. S. Gopal, ed., *Anatomy of a Confrontation: Babri Masjid and Ramjanmabhumi Issue* (Delhi: Viking, 1991). See in particular the thoughtful essay by Neeladri Bhattacharya.

9. See the discussion in *Provincialising Europe*, Introduction.

10. Michel Foucault, *Discipline and Punish: The Birth of the Prison*, trans. Alan Sheridan (Harmondsworth: Penguin, 1979), p.148.

11. The Arts Faculty of the University of Melbourne, where I once taught, routinely advertised the BA degree as one that made students employable by imparting to them the general skills needed by bureaucracies. For Foucault's ideas on 'governmentality', see Michel Foucault, 'Governmentality', in Graham Burchell, Colin Gordon and Peter Miller eds., *The Foucault Effect: Studies in Governmentality* (Hertfordshire: Harvest Wheatsheaf, 1991), pp. 87–104.

12. In referring to the idea of 'the multitude', I am engaging in an implicit conversation with ideas put forward by Michael Hardt and Antonio Negri in their book *Empire* (Cambridge, Mass.: Harvard University Press, 2000). But a fuller conversation must await opportunities for further elaboration of my position.

13. Illaih, 'Productive Labour, Consciousness and History'.

14. Ibid., p. 168.

15. Here also we must note that Ilaih's rejection of academic disciplines cannot ever be total, living as he does in structures dominated by visions of governmentality. Thus he must employ, minimally, some sociological or anthropological reasoning to find and identify his 'Dalitbahujan' constituency on the ground.

16. Badri Narayan, *Documenting Dissent: Contesting Fables, Contested Memories and Dalit Political Discourse* (Shimla: Indian Institute of Advanced Study, 2001). The expression 'historian's history' is taken from Gyanendra Pandey's recent book *Remembering Partition* (Cambridge: Cambridge University Press, 2001).

17. Narayan, *Documenting Dissent*, pp. 119–20.

18. Ibid., pp. 123–33.
19. One account of this debate may be found in the Indian magazine *Frontline*, vol.18, no.3, July 23–June 6, 2001. The prominent anthropologist André Béteille was at the heart of this debate and attracted much hostile criticism for suggesting that historical and anthropological evidence did not bear out the contention of those who argued that caste and race were similar, if not identical, categories. An essay by Yogendra Yadav published in the Bengali daily *Anandabazar Patrika* criticised Béteille's position as 'self-interested' and 'hypocritical'. See Yogendra Yadav, 'Barna, Jati o Kancha Ilaih: Antorjatik Shahajjer Mayamriga' (Varna, Jati and Kancha Illaih: The Mirage of International Cooperation), *Anandabazar Patrika*, September 20, 2001.
20. B.K. Nehru, 'Gains and Losses', *Frontline*, vol.14, no.16, August 9–22, 1997, pp. 74–5.

10

On the Advantages of Being a Barbarian

Sudipta Kaviraj

I deally, I would like to be taken as a Barbarian (in the Greek sense of a person whose language is unintelligible) but a cosmopolitan one. This is not simply being provocative. The first hope is that it will be seen that I have a different natural and conceptual language from my academic interlocutor, and a different cultural apparatus. However, the second hope qualifies the first. People like us should not, even for temptations of nationalism, exaggerate our difference with intellectuals of the West, since we are formed, in one very significant part of our intellectual deliberative life, precisely by intellectual influence from the West. We thus have much higher levels of ordinary curiosity than can be expected in any modern person in the spectacle of the West; we are formed and shaped by those influences, and by that history. But cosmopolitanism means at least two things: first the acceptance in advance of the possibility that your own culture can be inadequate, or fallible. Or, it may not have developed a particular skill of human creativity in a certain way. In that case, we should be easily prepared to draw upon the other cultures we know to give us a more satisfactory intellectual life. I try to emphasise these two things by teaching not merely Indian politics, but also Western political theory. Yet this cosmopolitanism is of a very complicated kind.

One of the most interesting features of intellectual inhabitancy in the modern world is that the West can be indifferent towards the rest of the world's cultures; but they can't similarly neglect the West. I wish to argue that this is grounded in the partly unfounded assumption of progress and Western superiority in everything, a strangely unsustainable intellectual stance. Though, equally strangely, it is held as a general framework of belief by an astonishingly large number of Western academics. This does not mean that, if asked, they would assent to this view; but their entirely comfortable ignorance about how the rest of the world thinks, though they primarily think about thinking, can be made intelligible only by this unstated, unreflective belief. I wish to argue further that this is considerably to our advantage, for the rather uncomplex reason that access to two cultures is, in some ways, better than one. Our presence as academics in the Western academy should, ideally, contribute to a dialogue. I think it is rash to be too hopeful about this in the short run: in the present state of the constitution of knowledge and the rewards that go to its various forms, it is likely that we will continue in the present state in which we know too much about the West, while the West knows too little about us.

My academic interest has been in three different areas: political theory, study of the Indian state, and study of Indian literary culture, apparently subjects without much connection. I have, however, felt over time that there are serious and subtle interconnections which actually drove me from one field to the next. I shall try to explain what each of these means to me, because in each case I think I have been forced to take an intellectual position which is rather different from the mainstream academic thinking on these subjects. I therefore would like to give a justification of how I see these subjects, and secondly, whether these have any seriously defensible connection except my purely adventitious liking for them.

The Present State of Knowledge about India—Orientalism and Political Correctness/ The Composition of Internal and External Knowledge

My impression about Western knowledge about knowledge about India is that it has made immense strides in one respect at the cost of falling back strikingly in another. It does not have to be seriously argued now that a great part of the earlier forms of Western knowledges about India were Orientalist in Said's sense of the term. There were, that means, at least three things wrong about it. First, it was quite often cognitively misleading or absentminded. Either it was so absorbed about its images about itself that it emphasised and usually exaggerated the difference between the West and the Orient, casually translating every bit of difference into inferiority.

Second, it admitted the existence of internal knowledges of those societies only if these found a place in a knowledge organisation produced by Western Orientalists. The pandits's views about Hindu scriptures were considered trivially arcane, but their information, reorganised by Western scholars, was acceptable. Thus there was a strong prejudice of Westerners knowing these societies better than their inhabitants. Finally, these cognitive inadequacies were never detected because this knowledge had another non-cognitive purpose connected to the power of colonialism. We can add to that a fourth bias: the tendency to neglect contemporary events in Oriental societies and a tendency to concentrate on its rich cultural history.

Compared to that kind of Orientalist knowledge, the present state of Western knowledge about India is certainly less tainted by Orientalism. However, I am deeply struck by a kind of double standard I come across quite often, at times in surprisingly clever people. There is a tendency among Indianists to treat Indians' work as nationalist and politically tendentious, while adopting a crass and unreflexively nationalist, or Western-dominant attitude in their own, and seeing their lingering pride in the British empire as the legitimate afterglow of a glorious past. I am surprised by the sensitivity of British academics when we speak about racial attitudes in British rule in India; surprisingly, even now imperialism is not seen retrospectively as a totally indefensible business. There is little understanding that just as in the West there is a kind of moral consensus against the holocaust, in India there is, understandably, a similar consensus against colonialism. Some academic work in India in recent years has sought to be self-conscious about that, tried to get out of that bias. Subaltern Studies history creates such outrage precisely because it has sometimes attempted to read history against the grain of nationalist thinking. I have tried to stress the need to step out of what I call 'the nationalist history of nationalism'. But two points should be made about this as well. The first is that because nationalism of a certain kind forms a kind of 'cultural habitus' for most of us, simply to say we should step out of the nationalist history of nationalisms is not necessarily to be able to do it. I am sure, despite our conscious or declared intention, our actual historical practice must constantly fall short of it. It is the task of our European colleagues to point that out to us without the pleasant and defensible dishonesty produced by politeness; and when it is done, we should not, on our side, react viscerally to that as the rebirth of colonialism.

Secondly, the resolve to relate to nationalist assumptions critically does not necessarily mean that we reject every one of them. I feel surprisingly unapologetic about Indians wanting to be politically independent; I find the general business of colonialism rather unattractive. And to prove our credentials as people liberated from nationalist parochialism, we need not adopt the Cambridge history resolve to show that Indian nationalism was inspired entirely by slovenly self-interest of the lowest possible kind. I can be critical and supportive of some nationalist ideas: I feel moderately pleased that we became independent of Britain, though I am not beside myself in joy with what Indian politicians have done with that freedom. I do not find the crass Namierite premises of Cambridge history attractive or acceptable. But I think today it is difficult to find advocates of that kind of post-imperial history among people in Western universities. It has become generally politically incorrect to be a supporter of colonialism, even retrospectively, which, to imitate a famous book on British history, 'is a good thing'.

Thirdly, the two great spectacles of Indian contemporary life, the one of poverty and the other of democracy, and the rather more complex wonder about how the two can stay alive together, have drawn a lot of attention in Western scholarship. This has, understandably, led to a huge shift in the Western academic output and curiosity about India. Instead of the earlier interest primarily in India's past, and what were conventionally known as Orientalist/Orientological studies consisting of philology, religious philosophy, linguistics, classical Sanskrit literature and drama, academic interest has been enormously redistributed, and the main emphasis has shifted towards social sciences: history, sociology, economics, cultural studies and politics, etc. This is a huge advance in some ways. It is true in some cases—mainly among lower levels of academic work—that, occasionally, traditional colonial attitudes express themselves—but that is generally a negligible problem: and such uninformed or unsympathetic writing should be answered more by ignoring them, rather than answering them.

But I feel this advance has been at the cost of something else which is quite vital. Although earlier Orientalist studies often treated the difference as inferiorised, they took the difference and some aspects of it quite seriously. One of the most serious, I personally feel, is the ordinary cognitive courtesy of registering that Indians have their own languages—Sanskrit, Arabic-Persian and the vernaculars—apart from the ubiquitous existence and convenience of English. The first step of taking someone culturally seriously is to accept the seriousness of his language. Sadly, this is slowly slipping in the new studies of social sciences. This can be due to several reasons, three of which can be specified clearly. First, often social scientists simply take on unconsciously the unheedingly universalistic assumptions of positivistic social sciences, and assume that the state either is or is not, democracy exists or does not; there is no sense in asking complicated and delay-causing questions like 'is it quite a state?' Secondly, more often, they simply find enough people with English producing enough writing in English to maintain the illusion that, given that they are reliably bilingual, the scholar does not have to know the vernacular. And finally, in some cases, scholars engage in painstaking fieldwork— not merely once, but over long years nursing their identical field; thus, even if they do not speak the language, the recurrent opportunity of checking statements of politicians against others, and checking statements against behaviour, gives them ample opportunity to test what they say. Anthropologists are the only branch of social scientists who, usually because their fieldwork is in relatively remote areas, and among people who often do not know it, and because they mistrust mediated reports, usually learn languages. But this I think causes an enormous problem.

Accessibility is not necessarily an antidote to intellectual prejudice. It is a truism that people in the West now know much more about the rest of world, if knowing means primarily viewing. But the increased traffic of images also means that they tend to provide more repetitive opportunity for reconfirming prejudices—in which the Western media, including the liberal ones, play an intensely active role. The task of academic knowledge, I would think, is to slowly criticise and counteract this ritual of self-congratulation.

Study of the History of Political Theory

Since Marxist theory is interrelated on all sides with other forms of European social thought, even to assert its incontrovertible superiority over other 'ideologies' we had to acquire some under-standing of other theoretical arguments.

More systematic study of social theory tended to show me that instead of what Marxists claimed about Marx—that his work was separated by an unbridgeable gulf from ideological theories before and around him—his thought was actually a part of a process of thinking about European modernity. It seemed that despite their enormous theoretical differences, most modern European theo-rists acknowledged that for some reasons modernity as a historical period was particularly difficult to grasp cognitively. Each one of them suggested a way of finding a process that was centrally causal to modernity. Each offered a theory of that particular process, which, because of the assumption of causal primacy, thus became a theory of modernity in general. I still retain my belief that Marx-ism is a most powerful theory in this group, but I have been forced to abandon the more orthodox certainty that it can simply, entirely unassisted, provide us with an understanding of the sociology of the modern West. It has to be complemented, in proper contexts by theoretical arguments from Hegel, Weber, Tocqueville, Dur-kheim, and others. However, this kind of enquiry forced me into another question which forms the basis of much I have written in the last decade.

In the case of people like me, the reading of these theories hap-pened always in the inescapable context of an everyday life in mod-ern urban India. Reading these theories gave rise to an irrepressible sense of both their familiarity and their distance: it appeared that things in my historical experience were both similar and different: it was essential to separate them. Schematically, I concluded that modernity comprised processes like industrialisation, secularisation, étatisation, and individuation, which were universal: but this did not imply that the actual events or end-states would be similar to the West. This made Western social theory indispensable and inadequate at the same time: that corpus showed us what modernity was and what was involved in making theoretical sense of it, but it was idle to expect that to produce a theory of our experience as well. I lost my faith in a transitionist theory of modernity: the belief that the European past showed us the image of our future.

But this naturally leads to another question: did not Indian culture produce some form of self-reflection on our experience of modernity? If it did, where was it? I felt we have traditionally looked at the wrong place. Theory is a form of reflection, just as poetry and drama are. For complex historical reasons, this form was not highly developed in Indian culture; literature, by contrast, was. It was hardly surprising that when Indian intellectuals reflected upon these questions, particularly the nature of our modernity, they did it through literary forms. I have accordingly tried to read literature, at least literary texts, with questions of social theory in mind—as in a study of Bankimchandra published some years ago.

Begriffsgeschichte

In doing *Begriffsgeschichte* I have tried to combine the careful, historical, contextual study of texts with the method of focusing on concepts that are central to the prosecution of a particular type of social practice, inclining probably a bit towards the latter. I tried this, with a slightly Bengali frivolousness, in a study of the idea of 'filth' and public space by looking at the history of a particular park in Calcutta. Personally, I have felt that the intellectual discourses we ought to study with particular care are the vernacular, since that is the theatre of greater intellectual and artistic originality. Often, the English discourse is produced by the same figures, but they are a pale shadow of the passion, argumentative force and eloquence they show in their own language. Evidently, when they wrote to other interlocutors in other regions, or about more general questions, they often wrote in English, and those texts and discourses have to be taken with the utmost seriousness. But we should not slip into the easy supposition that what comes out in vernaculars is inferior in quality. Happily, the idea that when Indians write in vernaculars they are more original than in English has got wider support, and young scholars have turned to vernacular material, often producing compelling studies of intellectual history. But other scholars find it impossible to admit of this possibility. Oddly enough, Indian education is increasingly becoming more monolingual than before, with the unfortunate result that academics trained in modern methodological skills often lack the more basic skills of a confident use of vernaculars. But in some ways the line of argument about enumeration of communities has had a great deal of support—both within India and outside—among scholars working primarily in history and anthropology. This in part is a consequence of the wide interest in Subaltern Studies, where this argument first appeared.

Study of the State in India

My second substantial interest in a longer-term historical sociology of power stemmed from the realisation that in the Indian context, unlike in Europe, modernity had been introduced by the power of the state—first colonial, then nationalist. The meaning of the phrase, 'primacy of the political', appeared to me in a much stronger and altered light. But the study of the state became infinitely tangled and deferred by a mass of problems. I became convinced that to understand both the effectiveness of the state, what it has been able to do in modern India, and its failures, what we expect it to do but which it cannot, it is essential to see it as part of a historical sociology over the long term. To understand the vexed question, how much has the national state taken over from the colonial state, it is essential to understand the state of colonial power. After all, all this is a study of modernity in India, and I became convinced that in India, if not in the Third World, the forces of modernity have entered primarily by the expedient of the state and its initiatives rather than by the unassisted causal powers of capital—however impressive it may have been in Europe. Even capitalism in India requires the crucial support of the state. We have to understand the state because it occupies such a large part of the story of modernity in India. However, the major problem is to work out a way of communicating between the disciplinary languages of political scientists and historians. By academic convention, political scientists did not look at the problems of political life historically; historians, by contrast, did not always ask the question about the global nature of political authority and its place in society, though they generated a highly detailed picture of political processes in society. I have tried to argue in works over the last decade or so that the major change in Indian modernity was not even the extension of the capitalist mode of production as much as the state mode of power, i.e. the primary change in India's modernity is the conversion of a society where order was produced primarily by religious authority to one in which it is mainly produced by the state. The entire story of India's modernity is how this society has become centred on the state.

The Study of Literature and its Links with Social Theory

I also have serious differences with others practising history of ideas about the study of literature. I cannot deny that my interest in literary texts is driven at least in part by my sense of enjoyment of literary texts; but I can now see a deeper connection between literature and my general interest in theoretical ideas. Modernity brings in a general instability of the most fundamental conditions of social existence, and in no society can it pass without causing the greatest, deepest intellectual disquiet. Some of the most important European thinkers put this disquiet quite directly at the heart of their theories: nearly all of them imply that modernity, because of the instability at its heart, because it is so difficult to equate it with any single social arrangement or state of affairs, is particularly hard to grasp and encompass cognitively. Although modernity, out of all social systems of human existence, is the one created as a result of deliberate designs and acts of human groups, it is also the most difficult to understand. It would have been utterly surprising if modernity did not cause similar disquiet in India, or Indian intellectuals did not try to understand its nature. However, every society applies to its great and most complex tasks those skills it has developed for a long time, in which it is intellectually adept, and confident. Indian culture did not have a pre-existing tradition of social theory; but it did have a long and distinguished literary tradition. It is hardly surprising therefore that the self-reflection of modernity that happens in Europe in the form of social theory does so in India in the form of literary writing. It is necessary to modify the hardness of this distinction, however. I think, in Europe theoretical reflection in the more abstract conceptual form was always followed by a commentary in an artistic-literary form. It is hardly surprising that contemporary historians of ideas, who have sought to understand the peculiar constellation of ideas Europe has lived with for the last three centuries, have often supplemented the chronicle of theory with a history of literary reflection, particularly the novel.[1] It is also noticeable that a number of theorists/social philosophers who are dissatisfied with modern liberal social thought have turned to the intellectual resources of the European past, a large part of which consists in philosophical reflection in literature. Again, in nineteenth-century India, intellectuals, faced with philosophical questioning from the modern West, similarly used the resources of their own tradition—mostly literature—to find reasonings, arguments, values, attitudes which they could recover and reinterpret. To study literature is not to move away from theoretical questions, but to find a way of moving into them in a serious manner. In the Western universities, there is not yet a great deal of work of this type on India—for understandable reasons. As I pointed out before, technical linguistic skills have gone through a decline; and there is a tendency, which I deplore, to study Indian writers in English as representative Indian authors rather than vernacular figures. But in a different sense, this in fact moves parallel to trends in Western writings on social theory, though, again for understandable reasons, Western writers writing this kind of work are usually not familiar with earlier trends in other cultures.

Theory: What is Post-colonial Theory?

But because of my primary interest in social theory, I would like to return briefly to the problem of theory of, about, from the Third World. Theory from non-European sources has been associated rather too tightly with what is now known as post-colonial theory. I do not respond warmly to it not because I do not agree with what this theory does, but because I am sceptical about its claim to being theory at all. There is hardly any doubt that those associated with this trend are extremely proficient with strands of contemporary theoretical thinking in the West, and write fluently in these idioms. But that was not the claim which launched this 'theory': that was to be different from Western theory. Now it is ironic to say the least to argue that the sign of breaking away from Western theory is to show great proficiency in it. It is undeniably true that their thinking or enterprise is theoretical; but they do not constitute a different body of theory. On one side, it represents a desire for a theory which is distinctive—which I am prepared to respect provided that this desire is not confused with the production of the theory itself. In some cases, the trouble is that in case of cultural criticism, the analyses are not so much of non-Western texts of value, but of Western texts dealing with the West. Thus, critics might produce scintillating analyses of sixteen unmindful paragraphs in Jane Austen or Wilkie Collins or Dickens where they write about India. Unfortunately, and quite simply, that is not equivalent to a study of six volumes of Tagore. I feel that serious and more worthwhile theory might be produced by that kind of engagement rather than of the kind produced by Said, which was essential, therapeutic, cathartic, but eventually not very central. It is a catalogue of how

Westerners failed to get something right, not of how non-Western-ers thought about anything at all. Paradoxically, therefore, my be-lief is that we can produce more serious non-Western theory if we think somewhat less of what the West has done rightly or wrongly, and what the present West thinks about what we say the past West thought wrongly.

NOTE

1. The list is too distinguished and long to really require mention: but the list stretches from Gramsci, Lukács, Bakhtin, Lucien Goldmann, and René Girard, to Charles Taylor and others today.

11

The Ones Who Stayed
Behind

Ramachandra Guha

When the British left the subcontinent in 1947, there was not, in the strict sense, an established social science tradition in the region.[1] The universities were few and far between. Research was not their aim; rather, they were supposed only to turn out lawyers and clerks and irrigation engineers. There were no serious scholarly journals either. Nonetheless, there were some individuals who defied the inhospitable climate of colonial rule to produce work of high quality. In Bombay, G.S. Ghurye was encouraging his students to conduct rigorous fieldwork while himself working on an enviable range of subjects: race, Indology, the comparison of civilisations. In Lucknow, Radhakamal Mukerjee

was pioneering the discipline of social ecology. In Pune, Irawati
Karve was beginning the studies of caste and kinship organisation
with which she was to make her name. Across the country, in Calcutta, Nirmal Bose was developing his idea of the 'Hindu model
of tribal absorption'. Standing out in this underpopulated group
were two scholars who were also institution-builders: the economist and sociologist D.R. Gadgil, who founded the Gokhale
Institute of Politics and Economics, and the physicist P.C. Maha-
lanobis, who founded the Indian Statistical Institute in Calcutta—
which, despite its name and the formal training of its director, was
from the beginning hospitable to interdisciplinary research in the
social sciences.

Research in the social sciences and humanities got a ferocious
fillip with Independence. There were now new universities with
new departments. New professional associations and journals were
born. By the standards of a poor country, the state was generous
with its funding. The quantity and, in time, the quality of research
increased markedly. Institutions such as the Delhi School of Economics set standards of research and teaching to match those elsewhere in the world. Scholars were encouraged and inspired by the
commitment of their political leaders to the spirit of democracy.
Unlike in other ex-colonies, there were no curbs on the freedom of
expression and movement. Researchers could go where they wished,
study what they wanted to, and say what they thought.

Fortunately for the new generation of South Asian scholars,
there were now three acknowledged journals of merit: *The Indian
Economic and Social History Review*, edited by Dharma Kumar
from the Delhi School of Economics; *Contributions to Indian*

Sociology, edited by T.N. Madan at the Institute of Economic Growth; and the *Economic and Political Weekly*, edited by Krishna Raj from Bombay (in its earlier form this was called the *Economic Weekly* and edited by Sachin Chaudhury). These three outstanding editors published essays on all kinds of themes: economic planning, agrarian structure, foreign trade; caste, kinship, social conflict; religion, party politics, electoral behaviour; nationalism, environmentalism, feminism. Alongside Ravi Dayal, who gave a pioneering impetus to Indian academic publishing as head of the Indian wing of Oxford University Press over the same period, these editors could call upon a bevy of first-rate Indian scholars who would write for them or solicit academic writing for them. Consider some of the people living and working in India in the 1960s and 1970s, the scholars whose names peeped in and out of the aforementioned journals. They include Romila Thapar, Irfan Habib and Ashin Dasgupta in history; S.C. Dube, André Béteille and M.N. Srinivas in sociology; Amartya Sen, K.N. Raj, V.M. Dandekar and Krishna Bharadwaj in economics; and Rajni Kothari in political science.

The list, naturally, is illustrative, not exhaustive. Other names could (and must) be added. What they illustrate is that, speaking of India at any rate, one could say with confidence that by the late 1960s there was in place a vigorous tradition of research and debate in the humanities and social sciences. It is quite mistaken to suggest, as the invitation to contribute to the present symposium does, that 'it is only in the last two decades' that work by Asian scholars at home and abroad has 'come to challenge past research trends and contributed to a renewed vision of these societies and cultures.'

These words suggest an amnesia that, unfortunately, is quite widespread. The increasing visibility of South Asians in the international (especially American) academy has led to the mistaken and ahistorical claim that there was no tradition of serious research before the present crop of diasporic intellectuals made their leisurely way to the West. The work done by Indian scholars of an earlier generation, it must be underlined, was theoretically subtle as well as empirically rich. André Béteille's comparative studies of inequality elegantly matched social theory with field materials. M.N. Srinivas provided three concepts that greatly aided the understanding of modern India: Sanskritisation, dominant caste, and vote bank. (The last of these concepts, indeed, can be used with profit to explore political processes almost anywhere in the modern world.) Radhakamal Mukerjee anticipated, by decades, the methodological alliance recently forged in American university departments between ecology and the social sciences. Years before any of us, these scholars were—if I may be permitted to steal another quote from the editors' invitation—'focusing on new questions, new objects, new approaches which—it might be argued—have contributed to defining new paradigms for research and to reconsidering the links between disciplines.'

A direct acknowledgement of the robustness of Indian scholarship in the 1960s and 1970s is how highly their work was regarded in the metropolitan centres of intellectual power. In the early 1960s, Romila Thapar was invited to write the *Penguin History of India*. A decade later, Dharma Kumar was asked to edit the *Cambridge Economic History of India*. Two women scholars based in India were chosen over a host of likely foreign contenders by these generally conservative publishing houses. More noteworthy still were the invitations to Indian sociologists to undertake projects that were not about India at all. Thus, M.N. Srinivas was invited to edit the posthumously collected papers of A.R. Radcliffe-Brown, and André Béteille was asked by Penguin to edit an authoritative cross-cultural collection on social inequality.

A second indicator of the 'state of the field' was that the best foreign scholars of South Asia wished to publish their *best* work in Indian journals. That was where the richest and most productive debates were. This is where you wished to be noticed if you lived in Paris or New York but worked on caste, or peasants, or deindustrialisation, or religious violence.

Since the 1980s, however, there has arisen a parallel discourse on South Asia. This is conducted in North American journals. The actors may be mostly of South Asian origin, and the subjects may nominally be South Asian. But the place of publication and, more importantly, the style of analysis and presentation makes clear that this is driven by the preoccupations of the American academy. Thus, in 2001, one can speak meaningfully of two quite distinct discourses: one conducted within India, one conducted outside but apparently on India. These discourses have different inflections, different theoretical orientations, different purposes. Also, for the most part, different and largely overlapping casts of characters. Indians living and working in India write primarily in Indian journals, while non-resident Indians and (increasingly) foreign scholars write primarily in journals published in North America. The separation of the two discourses comes home most powerfully when one reads dissertations produced in America, which often tend to be ignorant of relevant Indian literature in the field, while quoting to excess works of social theory which seem to have little bearing on the dissertation's themes.

One more pointer to this separation: the journals a scholar might choose to publish his or her work in. I know from experience how hard it is to persuade a young scholar based in America to publish in one of the quality Indian journals I have mentioned. Of ten individuals one asks, at best two or three might consider it, and then not for the 'meat' of their work, but for its incidental by-products. On would think that for a diasporic scholar working on topics such as agriculture and pastoralism the *Economic and Political Weekly* is the logical place to publish, for the journal is read by thousands of scholars, social workers, activists, journalists and bureaucrats. To publish in its pages is to actively contribute to a rich and sophisticated public debate. When such a scholar chooses an American journal in preference to the *EPW*, it is not difficult to conclude that for him (or her) 'India' is merely a re-source on the road to scholarly advancement.

There is some traffic of ideas, but only a little. The Indian jour-nals can be read by those in the West who are interested. However, the prohibitive cost of foreign journals means that, at least outside Delhi, no Indian student can get to read them. As for the aspiring scholar, he or she has to very quickly decide where his or her prim-ary audience must lie. For the two discourses are driven by very dif-ferent agendas. One is responding to the history and social debates of the subcontinent, the other to debates current in the American academy. The point will become clearer if one tries to compile alphabetical lists of key words. The list, for the Indian case, might begin with 'Adivasi, backward caste, communalism, decentralisa-tion . . .'. The list, for the North American or diasporic scenario, might begin with 'aporia, bricolage, cultural studies, alterity, deconstruction...' Likewise, a list of key texts and authors in India might begin with 'Ambedkar, Béteille, (the) Constitution, Dharampal...', whereas the diasporic list might begin with 'Althusser, Bourdieu, de Certeau, Derrida...'. The point cannot be overstressed: that one discourse is located firmly in the cultural and political milieu of the subcontinent, whereas the other discourse is deliberately distancing itself from that milieu.

II

I have provided what I think is a necessary historical corrective to the impression that South Asian scholarship was in a state of primitive empiricism before it was elevated by the migration of a few talented individuals to the American academy. I can sense the unease that my argument will give rise to—in some readers. Am I a defensive patriot or, worse, an unthinking nativist? Let me anticipate and answer these criticisms with a detour into personal experience.

I was educated exclusively in India, doing a master's in economics in Delhi (1979) and a doctorate in sociology in Calcutta (1985). My first essays were published in the *Economic and Political Weekly*. But my early scholarly hero was a foreigner, E.P. Thompson. I was attracted by his exploration of the forgotten figures of history, by the elegance of his prose and above all by his defiance of intellectual fashion. I first went abroad in 1986, to teach at Yale University. I have since taught at Stanford and Berkeley, spent a term at Oxford, and a year at the Wissenschaftskolleg zu Berlin. All told, I have lived four out of the last fifteen years out of India. What I have to say now stems from this experience.

169

As I see it, scholarly work in the humanities and social sciences basically has these motivations: one might be driven by the criteria of 'relevance', by the desire to influence policy by one's work, or at least correct the injustices of history by one's writing. One might be excited by an intellectual puzzle, seeking through research and analysis to explain a complicated social process. Or one might merely be following an intellectual fashion. The first two agendas take their cues from the wider world. They are both productive of serious and rigorous empirical research. The last trend is a response to the printed word. It is dictated by the journals or thinkers that are currently influential. Here, research takes second place to what passes for 'theory'.

None of these agendas are the privilege of any particular geographical location. Specific research projects may partake of more than one agenda. Over the course of their careers, individuals may shift from one style of research to another. Yet I would suggest that there are discernible orientations, clear choices made by scholars and, in the aggregate, by communities. Indian scholars are more likely to be moved by 'social relevance' in choosing their topic of study and strategies of research. European scholars are by temperament and training more inclined to seek out, and answer, an intellectual puzzle. And scholars based in America just a little more likely to be driven by fashion.

Over the years, I have myself become increasingly attracted to European scholars and styles of scholarship.[2] I have learnt much from collaborations with the historian David Arnold and the anthropologist Jonathan P. Parry. Both are fine researchers and more theoretically astute than British scholars have a right to be. A person I have admired for many years is the social historian

David Hardiman, a scholar of zest and energy and unswerving commitment. It is a minor scandal that, in the ongoing rewriting of the Subaltern Studies project, the absolutely seminal contributions of Hardiman tend to be overlooked. There was an essay published in the *American Historical Review* some years ago which purported to be a history of the Subaltern Studies project, but which somehow managed to leave out two of the movement's founding members. One was Sumit Sarkar, who was airbrushed out of this official history principally because he was seen as a heretic—as one who had too vocally criticised the descent of some of his colleagues into discourse analyis. The other was Hardiman, who was left out in the *AHR* essay because, I suspect, he is white, male and British: a triple disqualification nowadays in the American academy. How could an intellectual movement advertised as being in and of the Third World acknowledge the central part played in its making by an Englishman?

Moving beyond South Asia, my work on ideologies of global environmentalism has been greatly influenced by European scholars. Collaborative research with the Catalan political economist Juan Martinez Alier helped me develop the idea of the 'environmentalism of the poor'. Conversations with the German philosopher Wolfgang Sachs furthered my understanding of modern consumerism and its cultural components. The work of the Norwegian anthropologist Arné Kalland proved indispensable in understanding the politics of protected areas.

My appreciation of European scholars deepened over the year I spent in Berlin. Two of my colleagues in the Wissenschaftskolleg had devoted more than a decade of their lives to a single project. Nicholas Boyle, of Cambridge, was writing a three-volume life of

Goethe; Hans Medick, of Gottingen, was writing a long-range history of a single Swabian village. The two volumes Boyle has now published have assured his work the status of a great modern biography. Medick's study of Laichingen, published in 1997, was immediately acclaimed as a classic work of social history. The years of toil and struggle paid off: yet can one easily imagine their undertaking the task had they been located in an American academy? Would not considerations of tenure, citation indices, student assessments and the like have put paid to any such ambitions?

As it happens, there are a few American scholars who have bucked the trend. One such is Robert P. Goldman of the University of California at Berkeley. He has made it his life's work to study and translate the *Ramayana*. He is a scholar of depth and subtlety who is truly in command of his subject. But the subject, alas, is not currently fashionable. Indeed, it can too easily be cast as an 'Orientalist' project, an unpolitical and hence anti-political work of the kind white males tend to take up.

Another American scholar I greatly admire is Richard Eaton. His book *The Rise of Islam and the Bengal Frontier* is a classic. It starts with a puzzle: how did Islam most flourish in a part of the subcontinent distant from the centres of Muslim rule? Why did Bengalis convert *en masse* when the Rajputs and Jats, so close to Delhi, did not? Eaton learnt some new languages to find out. Still, the answer required him to make a detour into geography, agriculture, anthropology, religious history, and architecture. His book thus became a 'total' history. Yet it is presented in prose so transparent that it effectively masks the years of dogged and difficult research which lie beneath it. The illustrations, gathered from the author's fieldwork, are an added treat.

A third American scholar I might mention here is Thomas Trautmann. He is a superb intellectual craftsman whose chosen field is the history of ideas. When I came to write a biography of the anthropologist Verrier Elwin, I read with delight Trautmann's extraordinary 'biography of a book', on the making of Lewis Henry Morgan's book on kinship. I have been educated and entertained by his recent essays on the idea of race and the study of Indian languages. His little essay 'Elephants and the Mauryas' is one of my all-time favourite pieces of historical reconstruction.

I have singled out a series of white men, so let me complicate the picture by introducing a little diversity. A fourth American whose work has both captivated and influenced me is Eleanor Zelliot, *doyenne* of historians of untouchability and a sensitive student of contemporary Maharashtra who is widely admired by the scholars and activists of Maharashtra. The last name on this necessarily abbreviated list is Ann Grodzins Gold. Gold is the author of an acclaimed study of Rajasthani pilgrims. I have just read her most recent (and as yet unpublished) work, which is an ethno-history of the changing physical and moral ecology of Rajasthan. This is a model of empathetic and in-depth ethnography, its results communicated with uncommon grace.

Where do Goldman and Eaton and Trautmann and Zelliot and Gold figure in the canon of South Asian Studies? Judging from the country in which they work, the United States of America— not very high. Were they to enter a seminar room at the Association of Asian Studies meetings there wouldn't be the buzz that accompanies diasporic scholars ten times as glamorous but not half as accomplished. I venture to suggest that there are two reasons for this state of affairs: the style of their research, which is classical rather than contemporary, and the colour of their skin. For the demographic changes in the American academy and the rise of 'identity politics' have successfully marginalised the white scholar of South Asia. The careful empirical work and command of languages that was their hallmark now tends to be dismissed as 'irrelevant' (or worse). The need to appear politically correct, or to be in with the latest trends, has become paramount. These trends can have a painful effect on emigré scholars too. At least two Indian historians of my acquaintance have abandoned empirical research after moving to permanent jobs in American universities. Both wrote a fine work of social history, based on research in a dozen different archives. They have now taken to writing essays based on books ordered from the library. These essays are supposed to be exercises in 'theory'. For the most part, however, these are merely extended literature reviews, parasitic assessments of other people's works according to the winds of theoretical fashion and the canons of political correctness.[3]

The picture, of course, is not completely black and white. There are American scholars of WASP extraction who have likewise reduced history to the scrutiny of easily accessible printed texts. And there are Indian scholars based in North America who continue to do serious and subtle research on anthropological and historical subjects. To pick names, again for illustrative purposes only, I might mention Kirin Narayan's studies of folklore and Vijay Prashad's work on Untouchables, both of which have genuinely illuminated for me the India that I live in. Then there is K. Sivaramakrishnan, whose anthropological history of Bengal forestry breaks new ground in interdisciplinary research. One must hope that scholars such as these set the trend for the younger generation, rather than the diasporic South Asians who currently hold sway, people whose penchant for posturing and jargon-mongering greatly exceeds their capacity for independent and original research.

These scholars speak grandly of 'provincialising Europe' but have not acquired the languages necessary to do the job themselves. Consider, by way of contrast, the biography of Vasco da Gama written by Sanjay Subrahmanyam, a work of impeccable scholarship using Portuguese and European-language sources that does not choose to present itself as a reversing of the gaze or the provincialising of Europe. My own hope is that, in time, the diaspora will turn away from its current absorption with the self towards a serious study of the history and politics of the West. Or of other countries around the world. Exemplary here has been the work on the Chinese peasantry by Kamal Sheel and Prasenjit Duara, of Sunil Khilnani on French intellectual history, and of Sanjay Subrahmanyam on European expansion.

The founding fathers and mothers of Indian scholarship were always open to ideas and individuals from the West. They travelled extensively outside India with an open mind and an enquiring eye. For the most part, however, they lived and worked in India. They followed Tagore and Gandhi in believing that a commitment to one's culture was not necessarily incompatible with a creative and ongoing engagement with other cultures. Perhaps I should stop speaking in the past tense, for there are still many of these scholars at work in India, scholars old, middle-aged, and young. In Calcutta, individuals such as Rajat Ray and Sukanta Chaudhuri nobly carry on the great Bengali tradition of the teacher-scholar. Teachers at institutions such as the Delhi School of Economics and Jawaharlal Nehru University (JNU), specifically at its Centre for Historical Studies, continue to inspire their students to produce high-quality dissertations.

Admittedly, these scholars face major obstacles: low salaries, shortages of research funds, lousy libraries, political interference, and so on. Largely for material reasons, young Indian academics now are increasingly attracted to jobs in the West (and particularly in the US). Previously, it was only the economists who migrated. Now the historians and anthropologists are joining them. A tradition of humanistic research in India that goes back almost a century is under threat. I must confess to a vested interest in its renewal. There are also solid intellectual reasons for us to wish that the tradition stays alive. Judging by what it has produced in the past, it is of rather more worth than the self-regarding productions advertised as the intellectual achievements of the South Asian diaspora.

NOTES

1. An earlier version of this essay was read and commented upon by Rukun Advani, André Béteille, and Nandini Sundar. The usual disclaimer applies with more-than-usual force: I am solely responsible for the views expressed here.
2. The names singled out in this paragraph stem exclusively from one person's experience. These are the scholars with whom I have come in contact through circumstance and common interest. One could easily multiply this list ten or twenty fold, thus to more effectively make the point that there is an impressive depth and versatility to European scholarship on South Asia.

3. Some American scholars do have reservations about the trends I have here identified, but are reluctant to express them even in private, let alone in public. This is in part due to the contagion known as 'white liberal guilt'. These scholars know that any criticism of the styles of scholarship that run under the rubrics of 'post-structuralism' and 'cultural studies' would expose them to accusations of being 'racist' or 'ethnocentric'. However poorly founded, these accusations, once made, would be deadly in personal as well as political terms.

This is doubly unfortunate, because post-structuralism and cultural studies are trends of dubious intellectual worth, and because their South Asian proponents belong overwhelmingly to the upper class. In the American academy they might strategically ally with African-Americans. But they are far from being victims of racial oppression; nor, like the East European Jews or the Irish or the Ukrainians or the Vietnamese boat people, did they get to North America by fleeing poverty or persecution. One might even say that after the people who arrived in America on the *Mayflower*, the South Asian intellectual professionals are the first immigrants who come from a privileged background. They have gone from being élites in their own society to being élites in North America. Why feel intimidated by them?

In the eyes of their American colleagues, the diasporic scholar 're-presents' India much as the Vietnamese or Ukrainian emigré represents Vietnam or Ukraine. Some crucial distinctions are thereby overlooked: namely that, unlike Vietnam and Ukraine and many other countries whose former nationals now work in the American academy, India is (for the most part) an open society with a functioning democracy; and that unlike those other countries, India has an old and still active tradition of intellectual enquiry.

12

My Brothers' Keeper

SANJAY SUBRAHMANYAM

There is an impression, perhaps mistaken, that the last decade or so has seen an important shift in the relations between 'Eastern' (particularly South Asian) academic actors ors and the terms of 'Western' academic discourse on South Asia, as well as the non-Western world more generally. There seems equally to be an underlying hypothesis, to the effect that this newly articulated relationship has something emancipatory about it, freeing academic knowledge at last from the burden of colonial Orientalism, and permitting the writing of what some have rather cryptically and portentously called 'post-foundationalist' histories and anthropologies (Prakash 1990). Every age is naturally entitled to its own forms of optimism and even of hubris, however naïve they may seem retrospectively. This brief note, in the mixed form of a memoir and a few observations, sets out to question some of the more comfortable assumptions made with regard to these recent processes, and spread through both the widely used 'reflexive turn' in post-colonial studies and other forms of ego-history.

Since the early decades of the twentieth century, the phenomenon of South Asian academics working in the West, and influencing academic discourse on South Asia both in the West and in their countries of origin in the process, can be dimly identified: S. Radhakrishnan and (the part South Asian) A.K. Coomaraswamy are two of the important names that come to mind in this context (Radhakrishnan 1927; 1941; Coomaraswamy 1956). Both these authors drew upon and even reinforced Orientalist clichés on India, a fact that is now being recognised for Coomaraswamy but not yet for Radhakrishnan (Gopal 1989). To be sure, even far earlier, in the eighteenth century, there was the odd Indian to be found in Oxford or London, informing the knowledge and the translation skills of the likes of Sir William Jones, albeit from a highly subordinate position. But, since about the end of the Second World War, this phenomenon has come to assume new dimensions in Britain, with the presence in the academy there at various times of such persons as Sarvepalli Gopal (1953; 1965), Partha Dasgupta (1993), Kirti Chaudhuri (1978; 1985), Tapan Raychaudhuri (1988), Meghnad Desai, Bimal Matilal (1968; 1988), and Amartya Sen (1960; 1970; 1982); and then after the 1970s, it has eventually constituted a veritable, multi-faceted, migratory and circulatory process for a certain part of the South Asian élite, with America coming increasingly to take the central place that England had once held. Other countries such as France, Germany, Denmark, or

Italy, have always been minor and exceptional destinations, both for South Asian students, and for academics; Paris, for example, has probably been kinder to writers, sculptors and painters from Raja Rao to Raza than to academics from South Asia. It is also probably disputable in the French case, for example, if any of the small handful of social scientists, linguists and Indologists of South Asian origin has had a truly serious impact on French academic views of South Asia. It is instead quite noticeable that such fields as 'postcolonial studies', which have gained considerable ground in the US (as well as in Britain) over the past decade, have barely touched France, where the study of such subjects as Indo-Anglian literature remains a quaint, and methodologically rather old-fashioned, pursuit for the most part, carried out for the most part by groups that unselfconsciously adopt names for themselves even today like 'sahib'.

I must confess at the outset to feelings of considerable ambiguity about this process of academic migration, and the disproportionate importance it is often given in contemporary intellectual histories, both by those who wish to celebrate it (though often treating it, rather romantically, as a form of 'exile'), and those who rudely denigrate it, while often themselves participating beneficially in it (such as, most notably, Aijaz Ahmad: Ahmad 1992). The first of the social sciences to feel the influence of this migratory/ circulatory process was undoubtedly economics, since India (and to a lesser extent Pakistan and Bangladesh) has been a major producer of academic economists since the 1950s. The institution where I myself first studied, then taught, and with which I continue to maintain some links, namely the Delhi School of Economics, was an excellent point of observation from which to capture the circulation of economists, to the extent that a sarcastic socio-logist colleague, namely J.P.S. Uberoi, even once compared it to an airport lounge (cf. Kumar and Mookherjee 1995). The traffic, even if asymmetric, did run both ways. Almost two-thirds of the faculty, when I was a student in around 1980, had PhD degrees from abroad, a few from the Netherlands, and a good number from the US and UK. They included such persons as the eminent statis-tician A.L. Nagar, the mathematical economist and planner Sukha-moy Chakravarty (both trained in the Netherlands: Chakravarty 1959; 1993); my own research supervisor Dharma Kumar (who had most of her university education in Cambridge), as well as younger economists of the time like Kaushik Basu and Pulin Nayak (with doctorates respectively from the London School of Economics and Rochester: Basu 1986; 1991; Basu and Nayak 1992). The economics doctoral programme in the Delhi School itself was by then virtually moribund, and had in the course of the 1970s produced a mere handful of distinguished dissertations, by such economists as Bhaskar Dutta and Ashok Lahiri. The broad hint given to students, already while doing their Master's Degree, was that they should seek out scholarships either to the US or to the UK. Every year in the 1980s, I would guess that the economics de-partment of the Delhi School of Economics sent out between ten and fifteen students to various destinations in the West, and the sociology department a few of its own. A mere handful return-ed. A few really prospered in academics in the US, a good many joined international organisations (notably the World Bank, the International Monetary Fund, and the International Labour Orga-nisation), and an interminate number joined small, relatively undistinguished, institutions in the US and UK, where they have since usually taught a standard economics that had nothing really South Asian about it at all.

Even the more distinguished of such economists have most typically worked within the two standard paradigms defined for academic economics: either neo-classical theory or, in the earlier phase of the 1960s and 1970s, English-style Marxism, for which the Centre for Economic Studies and Planning at Jawaharlal Nehru University was celebrated. Indian economists already by the 1960s had the reputation for being technically extremely proficient. Fields such as choice theory, growth theory, econometrics, and most recently game theory have had substantial contributions made by Indian economists, typically located in the US but also in India and the UK. It is probably justifiable in this case to see the Indian élite as providing a fertile base for the international development of a profession that had pretensions to developing an 'universal', thus ostensibly culturally unspecific, set of doctrines, forms of reasoning and theories. Economics was dominated from early on in this process by English-language journals, with roughly uniform patterns of refereeing, and the close reproduction of curricula from one country to another, with the US, and to a lesser extent the UK, proving the obvious models. A very able practitioner of neo-classical economics in the 1960s was Amartya Sen, who consistently published in the most prestigious Western journals, and even during his years as professor in the Delhi School of Economics was often abroad as visiting professor. He probably served as the key role model for later generations of students from both Delhi and Calcutta, who followed with interest his later career at the London School of Economics, All Souls' College (Oxford), and then Harvard University, before his elevation to the Mastership of Trinity College, Cambridge. In view of all this, it is obviously tempting to compare Indian economists with computer programmers, or physicists, rather than with sociologists or 'cultural theorists'. Nevertheless, as I shall argue presently, the economist's place is a key one for explaining some of the phenomena that I am interested in.

In contrast, the migration of anthropologists, historians, or sociologists of South Asian origin was slower to come. The suspicion may even have existed, as late as the 1970s, that to settle in the West was a sure way for a South Asian historian to lose his or her influence in the profession. The most obvious example was that of Tapan Raychaudhuri, who had left a professorship in Delhi in the late 1960s for a readership in Oxford, and whose career had then entered into a long period of eclipse before being revived somewhat in the 1980s by a work that was appropriately entitled *Europe Reconsidered*, discussing nineteenth-century xenology in Bengal (Raychaudhuri 1988). Raychaudhuri did, however, supervise a number of important theses by Indian historians at Oxford, who at that time took their degrees in England with the explicit intention of returning with the prestige of Oxbridge as cultural capital to be used in South Asia. It was virtually unthinkable, among the generation of historians of the late 1970s or early 1980s, that they would make careers or find positions in the UK or US, even if they did their degrees in the former. The eccentric case of Ranajit Guha, first at Sussex and then at Canberra, seemed only to prove this point; for, by choosing these external locations, it seemed that he had lost his influence, though the later 1980s and 1990s turned this perception topsy-turvy. Among the younger generation too, this only began to change with the likes of Sugata Bose and Gyan

Prakash (Bose 1990; Prakash 1990). On the other hand, the 're-turning native' enjoyed a cachet in India, as we see with a number of examples from England, but also with, say, the late historian and academic mandarin Ravinder Kumar on his return from Australia. From his strategic position at the Nehru Memorial Library in New Delhi, Kumar exercised a considerable influence over academic appointments, even if not over new directions in academic research.

Thus, as late as 1980, the international division of labour was clear in several senses. Only economists of South Asian origin really had an international market. Historians and other social scientists (and also scholars of literature) usually returned home, with the 'value added' of the English or American degree. To stay on in India for doctoral research was however rare for those who had the choice, and examples like Ramachandra Guha and Neeladri Bhattacharya stand out in this context (Guha 1989; 1999). When, after finishing my own Master's Degree in economics, I discussed the question of where to continue my research, Dharma Kumar para-doxically insisted (despite her own Cambridge education) that it was entirely unnecessary to go abroad if I wished to pursue South Asian economic history (Kumar 1965; 1983). Partly influenced by her very persuasive and firm assurances that I would get all the material and intellectual resources I needed for my research in South Asia, I stayed on to complete my PhD in Delhi; only one of my exact contemporaries, the economic theorist Ajit Mishra, did the same, although some years later; other *kurta*-clad Marxists and Gandhians made their way to destinations from Cambridge to Canberra. Dharma Kumar's assurances were, incidentally, some-what optimistic, as finding research funding for work in the archives turned out to be somewhat difficult, despite her support.

For instance, when I approached the Inlaks Foundation for a one-year research and travel grant in 1984, I was told by the supercilious Italian aristocrat who controlled the purse-strings that I should have thought about funding before choosing a research topic that required work in Portugal and the Netherlands. Besides, the Delhi University bureaucracy did its utmost to delay my doctorate at every step. This sordid story of negotiations with 'academics' from the Department of Library Science who peopled Delhi University's Board of Research Studies for the Humanities cannot be told here; suffice it to say that it cost me at least six months of research time (Subrahmanyam 1987).

Once I finished my dissertation in 1986 and received the degree a year later (another of those delays typical of Delhi University), I was so fortunate as to obtain a one-year visiting position teaching economic history and economic development at the University of Pennsylvania in Philadelphia. The intercession of Dharma Kumar was crucial in this, as the post was temporarily created to replace the development economist Alan Heston, on leave at that time; and I imagine that a number of potential competitors for the position must have existed in the US itself. In the course of 1987–8, I believe I saw the winds begin to turn in the relationships that I have described above, between academic 'East' and 'West'. Again, Philadelphia was an excellent observation-post, as Delhi had been for other purposes. It was there, in that very year, that Arjun Appadurai (an early social-scientist migrant, who had however even had his undergraduate education in the US, at Brandeis) and Carol Breckenridge were planning their journal *Public Culture*, and organising a group on 'transnational cultural flows', by putting together a reading forum where such authors as Frederic Jameson and Aijaz Ahmad figured (Appadurai 1981; 1997). Gyan Prakash and Douglas Haynes, both former graduate students from Pennsylvania, were mounting their counter-version of *Subaltern Studies*, which eventually proved to be a dead end, leading Prakash to redeploy his talents strategically (Haynes and Prakash 1992). It was also the year that I met A.K. Ramanujan, a key figure for understanding some of the business of 'representing' South Asia in the West. My own first field, South Asian economic history, still enjoyed a certain legitimacy then, which has since been considerably eroded. It would be virtually impossible in 1999 or 2000 for someone in my position, as a fresh PhD in economic history from the University of Delhi, to get the visiting situation I obtained at Philadelphia. But someone in 'cultural studies' or 'post-colonial studies' would probably find no particular difficulty.

My initial reactions to hearing Ramanujan in the US (at the weekly South Asia seminar in Philadelphia) were, I confess, rather hostile. I thought he played to a kind of exoticist register, and that he occupied a rather larger interpretive space than he should have, speaking as it were 'for India' in the United States (Ramanujan 1967; 1995). This is reflected in some of his later essays, on such subjects as whether there was 'an Indian (Hindu) way of thinking'. But I later came to appreciate the originality of his way of doing things. For one, Ramanujan had quietly broken out of the mould that had been created for him. His initial mooring in the United States, as I understand it, was to teach Tamil (and perhaps Kannada) language and literature, in a somewhat superior version of what some people refer to impolitely as the 'language slave'. These are those South Asians, or Chinese, or West Asians, whose role is to provide language instruction as 'native speakers', while being paid a salary that is far lower than their American or American-educated colleagues who are on the tenure system. An unfortunate example of this at Philadelphia itself (one of several) was a brilliant grammarian, and scholar of Tamil, called V.S. Rajam, who never found a proper job, and eventually quit academics for computer programming (Rajam 1992). However, Ramanujan, like Velcheru Narayana Rao at Madison, managed to open up a place for himself as an interpreter of South Asian culture from a primarily literary standpoint, aided essentially by his talents as a poet and translator (Narayana Rao 1978; 1990). Subsequent generations of Kannada scholars, such as the late D.R. Nagaraj, criticised Ramanujan's translations because they overly literalised certain aspects of the texts, but behind their criticisms was also the underlying sense (which I know Nagaraj certainly had), that to translate at all was to capitulate to the West (Nagaraj 1993). And, besides, the few translations that one saw by Nagaraj suggested that he was not particularly talented in that field.

If Amartya Sen represented one pole as an exemplary figure, Ramanujan represented something that was almost out of the reach of everyone else, whether as a public speaker, or as a translator. (Parenthetically, it is amusing to observe Sen's attempts in the last decade to speak 'for India', using his charisma and public appeal to address complex issues from Indian history based on a set of sophomoric readings. The 'cultural studies' temptation is clearly a widespread one.) However, the new sort of exemplary persona for migrant South Asian social scientists of the late 1980s and early 1990s was neither of them, but a curious third point, which can be identified with the definition of the new domain of the 'postcolonial'. From Ramanujan, the new wave borrowed the idea of the need to speak 'for India', or indeed for a new Third World, over which some diluted version of *Subaltern Studies* would extend its domain. To this was added the new market of the 1990s, namely 'diaspora studies', focusing not so much on the South Asian migrants of the indentured labour system of the nineteenth century, but the post-1960s migrants whose children were beginning to represent a growing voice on American and English campuses, and whose funds have financed recent chairs in UCLA, Indiana, and Brown. The identity politics of this group has become a major motor in determining the direction that studies of South Asia themselves take in those countries. At the most obvious level, this was also a political battle, for there was (and is) clearly pressure from those who actually (or potentially) fund positions in universities, and who have their own agendas, such as the largely expatriate Sindhi capitalists—the Hindujas; but also a number of others. In order to speak to this new configuration, an academic equivalent of a Salman Rushdie voice has been necessary, one speaking about South Asia in a way that Western academics could not do wholly convincingly (on account of their very identity), but equally one that was not so deeply immersed in South Asia and its specific contexts that it would become incomprehensible to an audience whose knowledge of (and interest in) South Asia is, after all, rather limited. Even if one could clone Ramanujan, this would obviously not do for the end of the twentieth century or the beginning of the twenty-first century. He knew too much, and about the wrong sorts of things. A more appropriate figure for this new context would be, say, the former psychologist turned millennarian academic guru Ashis Nandy, save that his particular persona depends to such a large extent on being located in India, in order to critique the West from the 'outside' (Nandy 1980; 1983; 1995). Thus, the question facing the 'post-colonial studies' field today is to a large extent simply: how to Americanise Ashis Nandy?

Such questions are, in any event, specifically American and English (besides being Indian), and have virtually no direct impact on an issue such as the perception of South Asia in France. In France, the vision of South Asia has long been anchored in the holist versus individualist debate, which was the major preoccupation of Louis Dumont and his immediate disciples (Dumont 1970). Virtually no living Indian voice figured in this debate, save as fieldwork informants. The one Indian social scientist whose work was academically honoured in France through an honorary doctorate in the 1980s and 1990s was T.N. Madan, and one can see that this is a reward for his loyalty to the Dumontian vision (otherwise largely rejected in South Asia itself). South Asian history is a marginal, practically non-existent, field in France, and is virtually not taught in any French university; the recent honorary doctorate given to Romila Thapar is curious, for none of her major works are translated into French. It is only at the level of the École Pratique des Hautes Études and the École des Hautes Études en Sciences Sociales (EHESS) in Paris that it has found a place; the Collège de France, for its part, continues its determinedly antiquarian pursuits in the name of Indian history. Interestingly, in the case of the EHESS, this has for the most part been taught by foreigners, first by the American Marxist historian Daniel Thorner (between 1960 and 1974), and then myself since 1995. Thorner was brought to France in large measure through the initiative of Fernand Braudel, and I myself found my passage to France negotiated in good part by the late Denys Lombard, a specialist not of South Asia but of South East Asia.

South Asian history has a very small place in French academics, simply because it has long been believed in this country that the appropriate discipline with which to approach South Asia is anthropology. If the history of South Asia were taken more seriously, the French media would not give the place it does to a risibly dilettante figure such as Catherine Clément, who has emerged as the public face of modern Indian history for a distressingly large number of semi-academic fora. Since colonial questions seem, even in general, to have rarely retained the interest of French academics, even the staple of colonial Indian history that works so well elsewhere in the US and UK is here virtually a non-starter. With the exception of a small group of nostalgic writers, who seem still to believe that the French empire might have been constructed out of India in the eighteenth century, the bulk of attention has been devoted to finding that part of 'traditional' India that still remains accessible to anthropological fieldwork. Here, one can see that the Marxist intellectual influence of Daniel Thorner (exiled in France during the McCarthy era), whose main focus was on peasants and agrarian history, in a rather universalistic (neo-Marxist) mode, has really been minimal, his only major direct student being Jacques Pouchepadass. The relationship between France and South Asia being largely determined thus, it remains to be seen how South Asian studies in the US and UK impact on French academics, thus creating ripple effects of a tertiary kind.

But here too there are noticeable barriers, of which the two most obvious are the structure of academic courses, and the nature of academic publishing in France. As I have noted, French academic approaches to South Asia still preserve a noticeable autonomy from those in the Anglophone world. On the one hand, this means that only a very small proportion of French production is translated into English; but, on the other, it also means that virtually nothing on South Asia (or even partly concerning South Asia) is translated into French from English. Of the major historians of South Asia of the last fifty years, the books of only one, D.D. Kosambi, may be found in French translation. Others such as Romila Thapar have had articles (but not monographs) translated into French. So far as I am aware, only one publisher to date has considered the possibility of putting any part of *Subaltern Studies* into French (Diouf 1999), and no such project has yet appeared for the work of the best-known English historian of South Asia, Chris Bayly (Bayly 1983; 1988; 1997). This is for reasons that are obvious: there is no certainty that a market exists for such work since Indian history does not figure in undergraduate programmes in France; for the rest, publishing houses in Paris work for the most part in a vicious and self-fulfilling cycle with newspaper reviewers, television hosts, and those who are series editors. Thus, outside the restricted domain of specialists, none of the historiographical developments of the past two decades are at present in a position really to affect larger debates in France. To the extent that some spillover might be conceived, it would be in the area of 'globalisation' studies, in terms of the engagement of French theorists of the new international order with Americanised media and cultural studies, or perhaps as Latin Americanists and Africanists in France begin to engage at last with *Subaltern Studies*.

But still another concern must remain, even with respect to the Anglophone world. It is certainly my impression in recent visits to the US that a form of massive historiographical amnesia has begun to set in there. To say that one works on South Asia inevitably evokes a simple response: 'Ah, in post-colonial studies'. But what of the rest of South Asian history, sociology, and anthropology: the part that is not directly concerned with the usual litany of 'colonial knowledge', 'transnational cultural flows', 'hybridity' and the 'invention of tradition'? The truth is that, today, there is a resounding vacuum where studies of South Asian history in the long-term are concerned, in the US and the UK—something that the bulk of academics there are seemingly quite comfortable with. The same very limited and repetitive set of writings has found its way into nearly all bibliographies and course lists, and a visit to the textbook sections of university bookstores is instructive as well as somewhat frightening. At a recent lecture in Northeastern University at Boston, I found that students of South Asian history there had of course heard of Sugata Bose, Dipesh Chakrabarty and Gyan Prakash (to say nothing of Gayatri Spivak, Homi Bhabha and Ranajit Guha), but not of Irfan Habib or Sumit Sarkar, who obviously do not feature in their reading lists. And when those who want to work on other areas and themes submit their manuscripts to academic presses in the US, they find themselves nudged with greater or less delicacy into conforming to the problematics defined by the new hegemony.

Who speaks for whom, then? Is the suspicion that, in the final analysis, the emergence into prominence of a certain set of academics of South Asian origin is blocking the way for the publication, expression, and discussion of other views in the current American academic culture, entirely unfounded? Is it too soon, in the US, to talk of the emergence of a 'Subaltern Aristocracy', which has the near-monopoly of the native voice from South Asia in academics, even as Kevin Costner has one on that of the Native American in the visual media? Viewed from the sidelines, the spectacle of the creation of the new 'native voice' is one that is sometimes amusing, but more often disquieting. To romanticise it, by claiming that it has brought an end to the Evils of Orientalism, is convenient but less than convincing. Whether academic institutions in South Asia, located in Colombo, Kottayam, or Calcutta, have the resources to produce another set of views and theses, with resonances that extend outside South Asia, remains to be seen. Much depends, as historians of consumerism might tell us, on the duration of the product cycle.

References

Ahmad, Aijaz. 1992. *In Theory: Classes, Nations, Literatures.* London, Verso.
Appadurai, Arjun. 1981. *Worship and Conflict under Colonial Rule: A South Indian Case.* Cambridge, Cambridge University Press.
———. 1997. *Modernity at Large: Cultural Dimensions of Globalisation.* Delhi, Oxford University Press.
Basu, Kaushik. 1986. 'One Kind of Power'. *Oxford Economic Papers*, 38: 259–82.
———. 1991. *Economic Graffiti: Essays for Everyone.* Delhi, Oxford University Press.
——— and Pulin Nayak. Eds. 1992. *Development Policy and Economic Theory.* Delhi, Oxford University Press.
Bayly, C.A. 1983. *Rulers, Townsmen and Bazaars: North Indian Society in the Age of British Expansion, 1770–1870.* Cambridge, Cambridge University Press.
———. 1988. *Indian Society and the Making of the British Empire: The New Cambridge History of India.* Cambridge, Cambridge University Press. Vol. II.2.
———. 1997. *Empire and Information: Intelligence Gathering and Social Communication in India, 1780–1870.* Cambridge, Cambridge University Press.

Bose, Sugata. Ed. 1990. *South Asia and World Capitalism*. Delhi, Oxford University Press.

Chakravarty, Sukhamoy. 1959. *The Logic of Investment Planning*. Amsterdam, North Holland.

———. 1993. *Selected Economic Writings*. Delhi, Oxford University Press.

Chaudhuri, Kirti N. 1978. *The Trading World of Asia and the English East India Company, 1660–1760*. Cambridge, Cambridge University Press.

———. 1985. *Trade and Civilisation in the Indian Ocean: An Economic History from the Rise of Islam to 1750*. Cambridge, Cambridge University Press.

Coomaraswamy, A.K. 1956. *Christian and Oriental Philosophy of Art*. New York, Dover Publications.

Dasgupta, Partha. 1993. *An Inquiry into Well-being and Destitution*. Oxford, Clarendon Press.

Diouf, Mamadou. 1999. *L'historiographie indienne en débat: Colonialisme, nationalisme et sociétés postcoloniales*. Paris, Karthala.

Dumont, Louis. 1970. *Homo Hierarchicus: The Caste System and its Implications*, tr. Mark Sainsbury. Chicago, Chicago University Press.

Gopal, Sarvepalli. 1953. *The Viceroyalty of Lord Ripon, 1880–1884*. London, Oxford University Press.

———. 1965. *British Policy in India, 1858–1905*. Cambridge, Cambridge University Press.

———. 1989. *Radhakrishnan: A Biography*. Delhi, Oxford University Press.

Guha, Ramachandra. 1989. *The Unquiet Woods: Ecological Change and Peasant Resistance in the Himalaya*. Delhi, Oxford University Press.

———. 1999. *Savaging the Civilised: Verrier Elwin, His Tribals, and India*. Delhi, Oxford University Press.

Haynes, Douglas, and Gyan Prakash, eds. 1992. *Contesting Power: Resistance and Everyday Social Relations in South Asia*. Berkeley, University of California Press.

Kumar, Dharma. 1965. *Land and Caste in South India: Agricultural Labour in the Madras Presidency in the Nineteenth Century*. Cambridge, Cambridge University Press.

————. 1983. *The Cambridge Economic History of India, vol. II (c. 1757 to 1970)*. Cambridge, Cambridge University Press.

———— and Dilip Mookherjee, eds. 1995. *D. School: Reflections on the Delhi School of Economics*. Delhi, Oxford University Press.

Matilal, Bimal K. 1968. *The Navya-Nyaya Doctrine of Negation: The Semantics and Ontology of Negative Statements in Navya-Nyaya Philosophy*. Cambridge [Mass.], Harvard University Press.

————. 1988. *Confrontation of Cultures*. Calcutta, K.P. Bagchi.

Nagaraj, D.R. 1993. *The Flaming Feet: A Study of the Dalit Movement in India*. Bangalore, South Forum Press.

Nandy, Ashis. 1980. *At the Edge of Psychology: Essays in Politics and Culture*. Delhi, Oxford University Press.

————. 1983. *The Intimate Enemy: Loss and Recovery of Self under Colonialism*. Delhi, Oxford University Press.

————. 1995. *The Savage Freud and Other Essays on Possible and Retrievable Selves*. Princeton, N.J., Princeton University Press.

Narayana Rao, Velcheru. 1978. *Telugulo kavita viplavala svarupam*. Vijayawada, Visalaandhra Publishing House.

———— and Gene H. Roghair. 1990. *Siva's Warriors: The Basava Purana of Palkuriki Somanatha*. Princeton, Princeton University Press.

Prakash, Gyan. 1990. 'Writing post-Orientalist Histories of the Third World: Perspectives from Indian Historiography'. *Comparative Studies in Society and History*, 32: 383–408.

Radhakrishnan, S. 1927. *The Hindu View of Life*. London, George Allen and Unwin.

————. 1941. *Indian Philosophy*. London, George Allen and Unwin. 2 vols.

Rajam, V.S. 1992. *A Reference Grammar of Classical Tamil Poetry (150 BC–pre-fifth/sixth century ad)*. Philadelphia, PA., American Philosophical Society.

Ramanujan, A.K. 1967. *The Interior Landscape: Love Poems from a Classical Tamil Anthology*. Bloomington, Indiana University Press. Translation.

————. 1995. *The Collected Poems of A.K. Ramanujan*. Delhi, Oxford University Press.

Raychaudhuri, Tapan. 1988. *Europe Reconsidered: Perceptions of the West in Nineteenth-century Bengal.* Delhi, Oxford University Press.

Sen, Amartya. 1960. *Choice of Techniques: An Aspect of the History of Planned Economic Development.* Oxford, Basil Blackwell.

———. 1970. *Collective Choice and Social Welfare.* San Francisco, Holden-Day.

———. 1982. *Choice, Welfare and Measurement.* Oxford, Clarendon Press.

Subrahmanyam, Sanjay. 1987. 'Trade and the Regional Economy of South India, *c.* 1550–1650'. PhD thesis, Delhi School of Economics.

13

Recasting Women in the Publishing World

URVASHI BUTALIA

Years ago, when the dream of setting up a feminist publishing house began to crystallise in my mind, I realised very quickly that there were a number of very material reasons which had led me to think of doing so. The fledgling women's movement in India was preoccupied with many important issues, and on virtually none of these was there any published material. The handful of books/publications that did exist came to us—as much material then did—by way of the 'West', and were often produced by scholars who had spent the shortest possible time here, and somehow became the definitive book on a particular subject.

Not only was this material expensive to buy, it also forced us to ask why it was that we always had to be at the receiving end of knowledge about ourselves, created, often produced, or at the very least mediated, by the West.

The reality, we discovered over time, was of course much more complicated. The discrimination we, as feminist publishers, faced, came not only from the 'West' (a homogenisation I would question today) but also from both male and mainstream publishers and academics in our own country and elsewhere. Such discrimination had as much to do with the *content* of what we were producing, as it had to do with *who* we were and *where* we were located. For us—my colleague, Ritu Menon, and I who set up Kali together— it was extremely important that we be located in India where we had cut our political teeth, and within the women's movement from which we had derived much sustenance, and that we publish 'Third World'—primarily South Asian—voices. We wanted too to intervene in academic and creative debates in South Asia and indeed in the world, from our particular location, and with the support of our authors and friends. Feminist knowledge, we felt, should have its proper place within what we call the mainstream and the mainstream should have the openness, the space, to recognise and respect difference, not to hierarchise it.

Things were not so simple of course. There were many battles to be fought, both at home and outside. Within India and South Asia, we were lucky enough to have the unstinting support of women's groups and women activists. But there was a great deal of scepticism among our colleagues in the trade and among mainstream, male academics. They scoffed at women's studies as a discipline, at women's writing as a genre. Do women actually write, they asked; would people be interested in reading them? Would we find ourselves enough writers of a 'good' standard? Would we be able to sustain ourselves by publishing 'only' about women (more than half the population of the world, we had to constantly remind them!)

Eighteen years later as virtually every major publisher in India is in the process of setting up a women's list, we are no longer asked these questions. But there are other, more insidious forms of prejudice that continue to dog us. Academic writers who were earlier happy to be published by us now sometimes claim that they feel concerned to be associated with a 'political' publisher and would rather be with a more 'neutral' one. In many cases, the so-called 'neutral' publishers often happen to be Indian branches of major Western publishing houses and they bring not only prestige, but prestige of the kind that Third World writers value a great deal. To me, as a publisher who has always acknowledged publishing, any publishing, to be a political enterprise, this kind of dissembling was one of the most difficult things to have to come to terms with, although of course over time you learn to accept such things and be realistic about them. In post-colonial countries, recognition by the erstwhile colonial powers (and indeed by the West generally) still provides a kind of legitimacy, and there is no reason to believe that academics, even so-called 'progressive' ones, will be proof against this.

These problems were not, of course, unique to us. Feminist and women's publishing houses all over the world have had to deal with the kind of discrimination that attaches to anyone who questions how canons are made and defined. In the last three decades, some of the questions such publishers—among whom I count

Kali—have asked have been: how have particular kind(s) of knowledge(s) come to acquire the legitimacy they have today? How have others been marginalised? How, for example, in history, sociology, anthropology, geography or any other discipline, did the male, and the white Western male, come to be accepted as the norm? Why is it that 'macro' patterns and experiences are always given more value than 'micro' ones? And so on.

Because these questions have to do with the way hierarchies of knowledge and power are set up, they are replicated in all such power relations, whether they have to do with gender, or race, or indeed history and geography. Thus, if for feminist publishers in the West, the battle was to confront patriarchies and prejudices among academics and general readers in the West, for publishers like us, there were added dimensions. Not only did we have to deal with patriarchies embedded in our publishing and academic communities, but also with bias and prejudice among our Western counterparts, both male and female.

Let me try to explain: when we first started seeking out Western publishers to collaborate with, we met with considerable resistance. We were women, we called ourselves feminists, we were based in the 'Third World', and we claimed to publish in English, a foreign language. How could anyone take us seriously? In all fairness, I must mention that part of the resistance also came from the fact that Indian publishers were not known for producing quality material, but this was in terms of the *production* of books (something that has seen considerable improvement in recent years), it had nothing to do with their *content*. And this was where we faced prejudice. In the late 1980s, a well-known publisher in the United

States who was considering co-publishing with us, but wasn't really sure of our credentials, wrote a mildly surprised letter to us after she had been to a seminar on publishing where she had heard a US publisher speak about Kali. She wrote to say that she was 'impressed' because 'clearly your press is better known here than I had imagined'. And we had little doubt that had it not been for that chance encounter, she would perhaps have not considered the manuscript we were offering. We asked ourselves at the time whether we would have ever made a similar remark to someone in the US.

But this wasn't the first time something like this had happened. We'd been negotiating with a well-known academic press from the UK about a book of ours, *Recasting Women*. After some four months of negotiation, the editor turned the book down, saying that it was uneven—which is a perfectly acceptable reason for turning something down. But she did not leave it at that, and offered to help teach us how to deal with Western publishers and how to find out what kind of books they appreciated. *Recasting Women* (which we then published elsewhere) later went on to become a classic of modern history and continues to stay in print, both in India and the United States, more than twelve years after it was first published.

We've had similar arguments/discussions with publishers in the 'West' because of their insistence on putting 'India' into the title of the books they take from us. While we agree that it is helpful to locate the content of a particular book, we often wonder why it is that books that deal with, say, British history, or US sociology, never have to be thus located? There seems to be an implicit assumption that there is a centre and a periphery here, and the centre is located in what is known as the 'West'.

Because of our particular history of coming out of the women's movement in India, Kali has always had very strong links (in India and South Asia) with women's groups and non-governmental organisations (NGOs). We consider the production of books and pamphlets that can feed into women's movements to be an important part of our activity. As a result, we're often approached by— or we approach—international NGOs based in other countries, to work on collaborative projects where cost-sharing, or labour-sharing, helps both sides to produce material cheaply. We'd thought, mistakenly perhaps, that dealing with such organisations— charities, trusts, etc.—would be less hierarchical and without the baggage of power and history carried by the more mainstream and commercial publishers. But we realised that this was a rather naïve view—for the burden of history does not disappear just by virtue of having a different type of organisation. So, once we were told by a very well-known, and equally well-respected large NGO based in the UK—with branches all over the world—that they 'understood very well' what we meant when we said we would like to buy the rights to one of their books for India. 'All Indian publishers are pirates', the chief editor told me with a laugh, 'I have a lot of experience of India, so I know how corrupt you are. You can do the book but I guess it would be a mistake for us to expect to be paid.' Similarly, a discussion with another organisation, concerned with the condition of marginalised people and minorities, ended when their editor wrote to us indicating that they could not subsidise the book we wanted to do as that was 'not their practice'. At the time, we were quite taken aback at this—we had not even asked for a subsidy. Instead, they had wanted to come in on a book we were doing on dalit women, and the discussion was about how we could collaborate, if at all.

I want to mention only one other such instance to illustrate my point. I don't want to make this essay a string of complaints about how badly we've been treated by the so-called 'West'. We haven't. On the whole our dealings have been good. But this essay isn't about our relations with Western publishers, it is about the more important political realities that underpin these, and about how this affects what can and should be a free and equal exchange. Recently, we were attempting to buy South Asia rights for a title by an Indian writer, from a US-based university press. While responding to my initial query about whether or not rights were available, the US publisher asked to be informed, first, about who our distributors were. I was surprised at this, and asked if this was standard practice and would they, for example, refuse us permission if they did not like our distributors.

Here's the reply I received.

Yes, it is very important [to know who our distributors are] as Indian distributors are increasingly being brazen about selling Indian editions . . . outside their allotted territories. The response of the publisher is critical as they should 1. Make their distributors aware of the territory restrictions. 2. Correct the problem once they are made aware of it . . . We have, in fact, taken the necessary steps to withhold future agreements and or revoke the rights altogether with those publishers who display a flagrant disregard for their contractual obligations with the Press.

Hardly the most conducive thing to working together, this statement also displays, to my mind, the arrogance that comes from identifying your position as mainstream, and therefore righteous, and everyone else as being on the margins, and therefore crooked. Book distributors in the United States routinely violate territorial agreements, invoking, if publishers try to stop them, the Fourth Amendment, asserting that publishers have no right to stop them trading wherever they wish in the world. Publishers in countries like ours who are at the receiving end of this, can do little, and we know that the original publishers in the US are themselves quite helpless here. But we don't write them rude letters threatening to 'withdraw', or indeed taking what are common (and not necessarily desirable) practices in business anywhere in the world, and assuming that they have everyone's consent. In other words, there are unscrupulous dealers everywhere in the world, but that does not mean that anyone else functioning within the same geographical space should be tarred with the same brush.

It's possible to say that these are stray examples and that they don't add up to a general picture of bias and discrimination. And I'd say there is some truth in that—for as I've said earlier, on the whole, our experience of making an intervention in our own context and outside has been a positive one. But I think we need to remind ourselves that the patterns of power and prejudice that underlie the existing and historical hierarchies in the world have not disappeared. And we need to be able to recognise them when we meet them, and to know how to deal with them. For us, it has been an advantage, I think, to be clear about and committed to our politics, so that we know that if a particular relationship is likely to be one of unequal power, no matter how lucrative the deal may prove to be, we will refuse to engage with it.

I think that what I am trying to say by way of these examples is that for me, as a publisher, these encounters across borders raise certain questions: does the *quality* of knowledge, I wonder, change once it crosses borders? Some of these borders are biological, others are political and administrative. How and why do they impinge on knowledge? And further, is it possible, given the political and economic imbalances that obtain in different parts of the world, for voices from the 'periphery' to be heard in what is understood to be the 'centre'? In other words, how successful can the enterprise of introducing 'oppositional knowledge' actually be, in today's world? I don't have any easy answers to these questions, but within Kali, the fact that we publish in English, has helped enabled our work to travel into the international arena more effectively than that of other publishers who do not have a similar advantage.

And I think it's important to say too that things have begun to change in recent years. Partly I think this is because the world is becoming a smaller place, but partly also it is because of the growing presence, and importance, of Third World, and for us, South Asian, scholars in the West. So many of our academics, and indeed many of our creative writers, now live and work in Western societies, or visit frequently to lecture or participate in seminars. It is their voices, and those of travelling scholars and writers, that have helped to prise open spaces in the Western academy, spaces in which now 'different' voices—anti-imperialist, post-colonial, Third World, feminist—can be heard. And their presence and contributions have opened up spaces in which it becomes easier for people like us to operate. Also, the reverse has begun to happen much more: particularly in the field of academics, but also in the literary world, it's become increasingly important for Western scholars and writers to have their voices heard in our part of the world. And this, to my mind, is another positive development. For us, over the last few years, this has meant some change within Kali. Whereas earlier, we were quite clear that we would publish mainly Third World writers, with the occasional book by a 'Western' writer, now we are more open to publishing scholars who have worked on India and South Asia and who may wish to be published here. Of course, our priority remains 'Third World' writers, but we do feel it is important for us to be open to and respect difference, if that is what we demand in our dealings with other publishers and other countries.

I must add that as publishers, even though we have had to battle with bias and prejudice both at home and outside because of the peculiar nature of our enterprise, we are still fortunate to be much more privileged than others. By this I mean that we in Kali have had the constant support of women's groups in our part of the world, but also that we operate out of Delhi, which is the capital city in India and which therefore gives us all the opportunities and privileges which are attendant on such locations. And more, that we publish in English, which allows our books to travel much beyond the borders of India—and which simultaneously limits our reach somewhat within India where English is only one of eighteen languages. For our part, we try to work with other Indian language publishers so that our books are translated into other Indian languages, but we know also, that English gives us a head start over others who publish in, say, Hindi, Bengali or other Indian languages. Thus, we're constantly aware of the irony of having to work in the language of our erstwhile colonisers, a language that gives us access but also makes us painfully aware of the history of power that lies behind such access.

REFERENCE

Kumkum Sangari & Sudesh Vaid. Eds. *Recasting Women: Essays in Colonial History.* Delhi. Kali for Women, 1989.